CONTAINER GARDENING

An Easy Way to Grow Vegetables, Herbs and Fruits at Your Home, Even If You Don't Have a Green Thumb

EMILIA OLSEN

© Copyright 2020 by Emilia Olsen- All rights reserved.

This document is geared towards providing exact and reliable information in regard to the topic and issue covered.

- From a Declaration of Principles which was accepted and approved equally by a Committee of the American Bar Association and a Committee of Publishers and Associations.

In no way is it legal to reproduce, duplicate, or transmit any part of this document in either electronic means or in printed format. All rights reserved.

The information provided herein is stated to be truthful and consistent, in that any liability, in terms of inattention or otherwise, by any usage or abuse of any policies, processes, or directions contained within is the solitary and utter responsibility of the recipient reader. Under no circumstances will any legal responsibility or blame be held against the publisher for any reparation, damages, or monetary loss due to the information herein, either directly or indirectly.

Respective authors own all copyrights not held by the publisher.

The information herein is offered for informational purposes solely and is universal as so. The presentation of the information is without contract or any type of guarantee assurance.

The trademarks that are used are without any consent, and the publication of the trademark is without permission or backing by the trademark owner. All trademarks and brands within this book are for clarifying purposes only and are owned by the owners themselves, not affiliated with this document.

TABLE OF CONTENTS

Introduction 5
Chapter 1. Why Urban Gardening 7
Chapter 2. Vegetable Garden in Pot 9
Chapter 3. The Right Pot for Every Plant 13
Chapter 4. Tools and Accessories 16
Chapter 5. Managing Pests and disease 21
Chapter 6. Herbs for Every Pot 26
Chapter 7. Kitchen Herbs 29
Chapter 8. Benefits of Growing Plants in Container 36
Chapter 9. Container Plant Design 38
Chapter 10. Best Plant to Grow in Containers 44
Chapter 11. Requirements for Growing a Successful Container Garden 47
Chapter 12. The Right Potting Soil Mix for your Plant 51
Chapter 13. Plants for Year-Round Container 55
Chapter 14. Tips for Watering Container Plants 57
Chapter 15. Container Material 60
Chapter 16. Container Sizes 63
Chapter 17. Where To Place Your Container 66
Chapter 18. Fertilizing your container 68
Chapter 19. Caring for your Container Garden 72
Chapter 20. Vertical Gardening Technique 77
Chapter 21. Vegetables and Fruits for Vertical Garden 81
Chapter 22. Indoor Edible 86
Chapter 23. Balcony Gardening 89
Chapter 24. Rooftop Gardening 92
Conclusion 94

INTRODUCTION

One of the major things about container gardening is that it requires a little effort, and everyone can do it. It does not need a lot of money, a lot of areas to grow, or a lot of time to spend. Container gardens are comprised of crops grown in containers rather than in the soil. Filling pots or buckets of different sizes with a soil less potting medium develops an efficient, easily managed garden. As you grow plants from seed to harvest, the container requires sufficient depth and width to accommodate the roots and plant to maturity.

A mini farm design where a household produces fruit and vegetables in unique containers for personal consumption to help increase the earnings and health of its family members. Any kind of container can be used for vegetable gardening as long as possible. It needs to be large enough to carry the plants and satisfy their root systems.

A container vegetable garden could provide pleasure and fresh vegetables. A well-drained growing medium, sufficient water and fertilizer, and plenty of sunlight are essential to make the garden productive. Just ensure you water your garden almost every day, because if the plants dry out fully around watering, this may lead the plants to drop off their fruit or flowers. You might also want to use fertilizer every few weeks.

The main purpose of container gardening merely relies on the selection of choices made by the gardener.

There are just as many reasons for gardening as there are needs. With such a small amount of land, a few seeds and tools, and also some fertilizer, anyone able to spend effort and time can grow a wide range of nutritious and delicious vegetables and some fruit. Growing your own vegetables can cost considerably less than purchasing them, and the food you grow may be richer in nutrients than the equivalent products you buy in food shops. We live in a time when food advertising is all about cholesterol, protein, and this or that type of fat.

Gardening allows you to move away from this absurdity and come back to the thought of eating whole, nutritious, delicious food, as opposed to any "nutrients" that recent scientists, marketers, and reporters have told us might be best for our health. Likewise, in an age where many people are almost completely inactive, gardening is a form of activity that has a useful end product, and it does not require wearing spandex tights.

To those with children, gardening can be an excellent way to introduce children to the natural world and food production and preparation. At last, many find it just plan nice. Container gardening will provide you with fresh vegetables along with relaxation and exercise.

Most container grown vegetables have a decorative significance, and therefore, can improve your home. The use of containers lets you take advantage of the numerous microclimates in your area. Lettuce, for example, can be grown in a cool, shady spot, whereas heat loving plants such as aubergines can be sown in sunlight reflecting from buildings or patio surfaces that contribute to the heat.

Though there are many views that you can or cannot grow in containers, generally speaking, the most important factors have more to do with container size, sun, and soil quality and less to do with not being able to harvest particular vegetables in containers. If you have a large enough container, you can cultivate almost anything. For those people who are just starting out, container gardening can feel a bit overwhelming.

Chapter 1
Why Urban Gardening

Whether you're looking to save money, enjoy picking fresh produce from your own garden or to prepare yourself for an economic or agricultural collapse, urban gardening is an excellent choice. No matter where you live – in a neighborhood or in a condo in the heart of the city – you can enjoy the fruits of urban gardening labor.

Some people have to live in the city although they are country gals or guys at heart. But this shouldn't take you away from your desire to create a beautiful garden! Then there are others who are just learning about gardening but have yet to really delve into it because of limitations of city life.

You may have seen empty spaces in the city being transformed into gardens by community members or even rooftops being made into gorgeous green havens. You too can be a part of urban gardening and it doesn't have to be hard or expensive. I think you'll be surprised at how easy it is. And I know you're going to love your urban garden!

Before you know it, you could have a mini garden that gives you enough ingredients or veggies to last you through the warm months. If you so choose, you can even use growing methods that will allow you to produce food all year long, growing indoors in the winter months if necessary.

Overall, if you live in a building or a house that has a small yard (or no yard!) you don't have to be left out of the world of gardening. You too can save money and enjoy fresh food for you and your family!

Grow Your Own Fresh, Local, Organic and Safe Food

Every month on the news we hear about a new outbreak of e. coli in spinach or food poisoning or contamination or the dangers of GMO crops...

I believe food should be safe, delicious, healthy and available to everyone! But the only way we're going to get back to a healthy, safe, sustainable food supply is to take back control over our land and grow it ourselves. Just over a hundred years ago, over 90% of Americans lived on farmland. Today, only 2% do!

Over 82% of Americans live in cities! What if we turned our cities back into farmland, growing healthy, delicious, fresh organic food for everyone to enjoy? We can do it with the help of people like you!

Growing Healthier Communities

Urban gardening isn't just a great way to grow fresh, healthy food – it's also a great way to build communities, connect with others and change the world one person at a time. Studies have shown that communities that garden have less crime and residents have less stress and live healthier, longer lives. What if you started a community garden in your city that changed your neighborhood forever, even if you moved away once it started?

What if you could grow a garden that would turn into a legacy and change the lives of future generations? I'm telling you it's possible!

Make Your City More Beautiful

Another huge benefit of urban gardening is that it makes your city more beautiful. Imagine if every abandoned alley and yard in your city was filled with a gorgeous garden, blossoming with ripe tomatoes, watermelons, squash, cucumbers, peppers, kale, bok choy, fennel, dill, lettuce and fresh flowers! Would you feel better about where you live?

CHAPTER 2
VEGETABLE GARDEN IN POT

Vegetable Container gardening will bring joy as well as bounty. The simple pleasure of biting a ripe tomato while it's still warm from the sun when it is picked and eaten on the spot is virtually unbeatable. You can easily grow any vegetable in the container garden, and you can also save money by growing your vegetable jar gardens.

Even so, vegetable container gardening generally is as frustrating as well as expensive endeavor should your plants tend not to thrive and produce. These list regarding basic tips connect with most produce and will let you and your plants be off to a good start.

Sun -- Most produce needs full sun – meaning at very least six hours of sunlight a day. It is easy to overestimate just how much sun a region really receives, so either get your clock out and time how long the sun hits the location where you want to put your vegetable jar garden or start using a sun calculator to acquire a general assessment.

Water – Raising vegetables will need water - a great deal of it. Even so, you don't need to drown your plants. The goal is usually to keep your soil moist but not wet. To figure out if your plants will need water, stick your finger on to the land about an inch down, or past your first knuckle. If your soil feels dry, add water. In case you're not sure, wait and check later in the day. With the heat in summer, you probably have to water at least one time, sometimes two times, a day. Proper watering will be the single biggest and hardest portion of vegetable jar gardening.

Heat – In the event you live in the really warm zone maybe you have to shade your plants in the middle of the day in order not to fry them. Also, it's best not to utilize metal containers or darkish colored pots or ceramics, simply because they can warm up and bake your plant's resources.

On the flip side, many plants don't like cold land, so be sure not to set your organic container home gardens outside full-time until you know this temperature are adequately warm most of the time. For a lot of plants this soil should be at very least 60°F. Check the temperature with a meat thermometer. If you're moving your plants from indoors to outdoors, you should do it gradually so that the plants don't suffer a shock from the change in temperature.

Soil-- Quality planting mediums are vital for fruit and vegetables. Don't utilize soil from a garden, because doing so will compact in your container and also won't drain water correctly. Also, one of the reasons to be able to garden within containers can be so you won't experience weeds. Chances are pretty good that if you utilize garden dirt, you will likely be importing weeds straight into your pot. I utilize organic planting medium because studies show we now have many advantages to increasing produce organically, including better taste along with a higher percentage of antioxidants and also phytochemicals.

Fertilizer-- Plants need to have food to be able to thrive, and their foodstuff is fertilizer. If the soil doesn't possess fertilizer already mixed in, you'll wish to add fertilizer. I use a natural granular fertilizer and also mix the item into my containers from top to bottom. Every couple of weeks I can add diluted fruit juice, fish emulsion or liquid seaweed to present them the nutrition they need.

Another great way to add fertilizer through the growing season should be to make or buy compost tea.

Drainage-- Drainage is key to not drowning your plants. You want your container or pot to make it possible for excess water to drain out of their bottom. Simply put, plants will not do well within water or soggy dirt. Make sure your pot has one particular large drain hole or a number of smaller ones. You can drill holes in the bottom of the pot should the drainage be insufficient.

Containers – Picking a container is usually daunting. You can use almost anything for a garden planter provided that it is actually big enough and possesses good drainage. Remember though, the larger the container, the easier it'll be to sustain. The morel soils a container holds the more moisture it will eventually retain. I particularly enjoy wooden canisters for increasing vegetables.

I like how they look, and you'll get truly good-sized canisters that aren't very costly, or you can make your own. Mine usually are cedar and also hopefully will last for a long time, provided I am careful.

Growing fruit and vegetables in self-watering canisters works splendidly well… most of the time. Problems arise after you get plenty of rain. Unless you do have a container where excess water doesn't drain easily, your plants can wind up drowning. Regardless, most of the time, self-watering containers are good at offering optimal levels of water. They can also be a big help for those who can't water every single day.

Plastic or glazed ceramic canisters are good too. Some people traditionally use terracotta, but it is harder to keep your soil moist in them because the clay will suck water out of your soil. To solve this problem, put a dish under your ceramic container and fill it with water instead of watering from the top.

For an inexpensive container get a five-gallon plastic bucket on the hardware store or make a container from something you have around your own home, such as a vintage laundry basket or perhaps a toy bin. As long as it's big enough and possesses good drainage, it is possible to really utilize anything.

Seeds or Seedlings – You can start your produce from seed or buy seedlings. There are some significant pros and cons to either choice. Starting your own seeds is quite a bit less pricey than getting seedlings, if you start from seeds, you can be certain that they were grown organically. Even so, starting plant seeds isn't for everyone. You absolutely cannot let them dry or they are toast. Then again, if you overwater them, they can drown. To avoid this, you can create a self-watering seed starter. There are also some common seed planting mistakes to avoid, such as burying your seeds too deep in the ground and putting them outside before the final frost. Make sure you read the instructions on the packet and don't plant your seeds too close together.

Simple Vegetables: The following is a list of veggies that are easy to grow.

- Tomatoes
- Carrots
- Cucumbers
- Radishes
- Eggplant
- Summer squash or zucchini Vegetables which has a high level of difficulty:
- Large melons
- Corn
- Large pumpkins and winter squash

Chapter 3
The Right Pot For Every Plant

Containers come in all sorts of shapes, sizes and at a wide variety of costs. They can be made of a many different materials and it depends on what you are growing, how big it is going to be when mature and where you are growing it as to which type of pot you choose. A heavy resin pot is not going to be suitable for fixing to a rickety fence, but it will be fine outside your door on the ground.

Budget is also a key factor in choosing containers as they can be very expensive, particularly when ornately decorated. However, you can make your own containers out of recycled materials or you can often obtain them for free through sites like Freecycle and Craigslist. You can even build your own containers out of brick or wood if you desire.

At the end of the day, the containers are going in your garden and need to be something that you like to look at and are functional.

If you are buying containers then there are a huge number of materials that your containers could be made out of. Pots come in all sorts of shapes and sizes from plastic to wooden to clay to resin to metal and more. You can buy plain pots or even ornate, decorated pots; it is entirely up to you!

Container Size Matters

One major factor to consider when choosing containers is the size. You need to be able to move it when it is empty but if you wish to move the container when it is full then you need to consider the weight of a filled container. If you are planning on moving it around then you will need to put it on wheels or find another way of moving it.

Larger pots are necessary if you are growing vegetables like tomatoes and potatoes that have large root balls, so needing more space to "spread out". Larger pots also provide you the opportunity to plant more vegetables in them, particularly when using a quality soil mix.

If you are planning on growing root vegetables like carrots or potatoes then you will need a deeper container than if you were planning on growing shallow rooted vegetables like onions or radishes.

Choose the Right Material For Long Lasting Containers

The choice of material will influence how long the container is going to last and how often you will need to water it. Porous materials such as clay dry out faster than containers made of wood or plastic and will fracture in a frost which shortens their lifetime.

Wood makes for an excellent material for containers, but it does have a finite lifespan. Rot resistant woods like redwood or cedar will last for up to ten years though softer woods may only last a year or two. Also make sure that you do not use wood that has been coated with preservatives, or that if you do it is one that is safe for use with edible crops. Many preservatives will leach chemicals into the soil, which can get into the food you eat.

You can use polypropylene bags for growing vegetables in. These are great because they are breathable, long lasting and come in a wide variety of depths and sizes. These can be folded flat when not in use and moved around your garden as you need them. Sure, they are not the most attractive option, but they are relatively cheap and easy!

Drainage Is Vital for Healthy Plants

Whatever containers you decide to use, drainage needs to be one of your main considerations. If the containers do not have suitable drainage then your plants are going to struggle to thrive as the soil becomes too moist and the roots may end up rotting. Most plants really object to having their "feet" in water and most will die if their roots are wet for too long.

If the containers you are buying do not have sufficient drainage holes then do not despair, you can drill them in the container yourself with most container materials. Stone pots are the exception as you are unlikely to be able to drill through them, but all other types of material you should be able to drill through okay.

If the container does have drainage holes then make a judgement call as to whether there is enough of them of not. In a small container a single hole will be fine but in a larger pot it will not and you will have to drill more holes. Also think about the plants you are putting in that container. If they prefer free draining soil then you will need more drainage than for plants which need moister growing conditions.

Some people suggest putting a saucer under the pots to catch excess water. These are okay to use if you are growing indoors so long as you pour the excess water out of the saucer after watering; they stop water damaging whatever surface the container is on.

Outdoors though it is a different story because sitting your container in a saucer full of water is exactly the same as overwatering the plant. By all means use a saucer but after you have watered your plant and the water has filled the saucer, empty the saucer. Obviously with larger pots this is going to be almost impossible if you cannot move the pot, but you cannot leave it sitting in water.

You need to think carefully about the type of material your containers are made out of because it will influence how your garden looks and where you site your containers. There is a huge variety of different containers available in any of your local garden stores and a walk around one of these will inspire you to create a beautiful container garden or you can make your own from recycled and reused materials.

Chapter 4
Tools and Accessories

Gardening can be done in several ways, but if you have chosen a container garden, you should have specific gardening tools for you to succeed. If you intend to acquire the most substantial part of your crops, you need to begin the planning before time. Purchase your seeds and garden equipment so that there will be time to sprout and germinate seeds.

Numerous gardening tools could be purchased, but the following are the essential tools for container gardening:

Small shovel:

A small shovel is perfect for pots. It makes it simple to dig in fertilizers and also to plant your crops or seeds in the pot.

Hand Weeder:

A hand weeder is a small fork class of tool with a long neck. It's useful for planting seeds and small plants and removing the little weeds that grow in containers. It can be used to dig a tiny hole to put the plant or seed.

Plant containers:

A plant container is a container for the crops, and it has to be the right size. You can make use of any container for growing plants and vegetable crops. Wooded boxes or crates, gallon-sized coffee cans, old washtubs, as well as five-gallon buckets can be used for growing vegetables in as much as there is sufficient drainage.

Small cups or egg Cartons to start seeds:

You can use this for sprouting seeds. Ascertain your container is sufficiently broad to give room for the seeds to germinate. If you do not have enough space, the plants have to be transplanted as they grow. Also, you may need to buy a seed heating device as most times you a required to sprout them within, for it to be adequately warm so that they can germinate and grow.

Soil:

Quality potting soil is a determinant for your plants to grow well. That is the secret to a successful container garden. If you use poor soil, your plants or seeds will not grow. The soil means a lot. Make sure you get top quality soil that your plants require to thrive with or without fertilizer.

Plant seeds:

A plant seed can be flower or vegetable seeds. The ideal thing is to look for high-quality seeds if you are to plant vegetables to be able to harvest seeds and keep for another season. Determinate tomatoes and shrub type plants grow brilliantly well in containers. If you're looking forward to the best crops in your pots, go for these types of plants.

Garden Gloves:

Though garden glove may not be very essential if you are the type that easily got disgusted by dirt and didn't want stain beneath your nails, or sensitive to some particular plants, you need garden gloves. Also, if you do not want to lay your hand on a caterpillar, tomato hornworm, snail and gardens insects when removing them from your favorite crops, garden gloves do the job better. It will also guard your hands against thorns or all other sharp components of the plants.

Watering can:

Watering can do the job better by making the task of watering plants simple and trouble-free because water is running out of it in the form of trickling rain. You can, however, make use of a milk jug to convey water outside. But if you are to use it, ensure you gently pour the water in your hand and spread with your fingers to enable the water to scatter and drop softly into the soil. If not, water coming from jug may land heavily on the soil and splash back on the crop's foliage, raising its danger of having fungus issues and other infections.

Trowel:

A trowel is also an essential tool for container gardening. It is being used to loosen up compressed dirt as well as digging through trash in plant containers. Rather than using your hands, the trowel will get the task done better and faster and leave your hand dirt free.

Pruners:

A pruner is useful for cutting off dead foliage and pruning plants. Though you might think of using scissors, it is not advisable to use it. There are wet saps on plants which may leave remains stick and rust on your scissors. Cutting plants with scissors instead of pruner also increase the risk of the plants being infected. Pruner is more active in cutting thicker crop stems, also enable clean cut while leaving your plants healthier in the containers.

Plant Organic Pesticide:

If you are a non-fastidious type who could squish insects and not have a bad feeling, a pesticide may not be necessary for you. However, if the reverse is the case, it is ideal you have a plant-safe pesticide as part of your tools. Ensure you adhere to all instructions on its usage because it may not be right on food plants. Possibly, you can remove the pest from the plants and spray on the floor with the pesticide.

Stick or String:

These are essential for supporting container plants that needed to be upheld. An example is tomato plants (string and stick or tomato cage can be used to support tomatoes). They can also be used for young trees that needed to be upheld to grow in a straight line up and plants growing up the fence. Stick can be bought at your local garden store. String or yarn could be an organic color, like brown or dark green for it not to stand out in the garden environment.

Quality Fertilizer:

Fertilizer is also essential for the growth of your plant. Having secured good soil, ensure you obtain a high-quality organic fertilizer to get the best result from crops. Compost can be in pellet or liquid form. You can buy specific fertilizer for each type of your plants like rose or citrus fertilizer. However, an all-purpose plant fertilizer does the job for most gardeners. Compost can as well be used to supplement your crop's feeding

Potting Bench:

A potting bench is also an essential tool for gardeners. Firstly, it serves as a platform to assemble and store your small appliances, plant marker, fertilizer, and the likes. You can also use it to conveniently move your planting tools from one place to another (for example, from your kitchen to your garden)

Each of the gardening tools is very important for your container garden to be successful. Make sure have them at your disposal to ease work as well as getting the best results out of your products.

CHAPTER 5
MANAGING PESTS AND DISEASE

Pest control is one of the more controversial topics with gardening, because pest control is typically the reason that people are motivated to use chemicals and pesticides. When pests are left unchecked, they can cause damage to the plants and prevent the vegetables from growing. Or, if the vegetables are already growing, then the pests might start to eat the vegetables.

Types of Garden Pests

Some types of pests are visible to the naked eye, and other pests cannot be seen by just looking at the plant. When it comes to pest control, it is best to be proactive to prevent the pests, because prevention is much easier than getting rid of pests that have already arrived.

Examples of garden pests include grubs, ants, fire ants, chiggers, fleas, ticks, beetles, weevils, flies, cats, rabbits, dogs, earwigs, fungi, deer, gnats, moles, slugs, snakes, and many more.

As this is a large subject in itself, we have a whole guide dedicated to it. Simple & Effective Organic Pest Control for Your House & Garden is a comprehensive guide that covers everything you need to know to find solutions for the exact problems that you are facing. Below are some of the more common problems and solutions.

Organic Pest Control Options

Even though pests are inevitable, there are a few natural methods that can be used to get rid of the pests. Many people think that they need to reach for a chemical pest control product, but there is no reason to use those unnatural products when the natural solutions work just as well.

Floating Plant Cover

1. Floating Plant Covers: Lightweight translucent fabric can be placed over the plants to act as a literal barrier between the plants and the bugs. This fabric is not a long-term pest control solution, but it can be a great option if you need to protect your plant during critical growth periods, such as during seeding time or when a specific type of pest is most active.

2. Bacillus Thuringiensis: This naturally occurring bacterium is found in the soil, and you can add more BT to repel many types of pests. There are several types of BT to choose from, and you need to select the type that is designed for the specific pest that you find in your garden.

3. Insecticidal Soap: A product with insecticidal soap contains compounds that are derived from the fat of certain animals, and the long-chain fatty acids within the fat can kill certain insects. When the insect comes in contact with the soap, it causes their skin to dissolve. The insect must come in contact with the liquid form of the soap; it does not work once the soap has dried. Also, be cautious, because insecticidal soap can cause burns on some plants.

4. Sticky Traps: A piece of material with a sticky surface is a great way to capture insects that are attracted to a certain color. When the insect flies into the trap, it gets stuck and cannot get free.

5. Pheromone Traps: There are certain smells that are emitted by pests, in order to lure the opposite sex for mating. Scientists have found a way to duplicate some of these smells, and the pheromones cause the insects to be lured toward the trap. Keep in mind that these traps usually only catch the males, which means that the females are still running free in your garden. If you find that you are catching a lot of bugs in your pheromone trap, then it is a good sign that you should start implementing other pest control methods as well.

6. Oil Spray: When you spray a pest directly with horticultural oil, it can cause the insect to suffocate. This oil can also be applied to spores and pest eggs, to suffocate them before they hatch.

7. Peppermint: Put 20 to 30 drops of peppermint essential oil into a spray bottle and dilute it with water. Shake the bottle well before using and spray it along the garden and on the plants. The peppermint is a repellant to many types of pests including insects and small rodents. It needs to be applied often, because it will wash away after watering.

Natural Fungicide Recipe

If you are struggling with fungicide problems, then there are a few natural remedies that you can try to get rid of the fungus. One of the easiest recipes uses apple cider vinegar:

Add 2 tablespoons of vinegar to a gallon of water. Put it in a spray bottle and spray the affected area every few days until the fungus problem is gone. Be careful, because the vinegar could potentially kill the plant, so you should use it very sparingly and only on the areas that are experiencing the fungus problems.

Weed Control

Controlling the weeds is an important part of maintaining your garden on an ongoing basis, because weed overgrowth can suffocate your plants. If you feel as though you are excelling at growing weeds, but your plants are suffering, then you might consider some of these natural weed-control options.

Keep in mind that the weeds are not as much of a problem once your vegetable plants are well established. You still need to make sure that you are weeding regularly, but the plants are at a lower risk of suffocating from the weeds once the plants have a solid root system in place.

The Worst Vegetable Garden Weeds

There are two types of weeds that might pop up in your garden: annual and perennial weeds. The perennial weeds are the worst types because, if you do not get them under control, they will grow back every year. The weeds come up and then drop their seeds in the dirt, which remain dormant throughout the winter months and then start growing again in the spring. This problem occurs over and over again each year, especially if you do not pull the weeds before the seeds are dropped.

On the other hand, annual weeds can be difficult in their own way, because they grow and spread very quickly. Once they start to grow, it seems as though they take over the garden overnight.

Whether you are finding annual or perennial weeds, it is important that you take care of the weed problem as quickly as possible, in order to prevent bigger problems.

Organic Weed Control Options

One of the easiest and most effective forms of weed control is mulching. When mulch is laid down between the plants, it blocks the weeds from popping up, and you do not have to weed very often.

Another natural weed control option is household vinegar. If the weeds are young, they will die when they are sprayed with vinegar, although it is not quite as effective on weeds that are well established in your garden. For the best results, you might need to apply the vinegar several times, in order to get enough acidity to kill the weed. Watch where you spray, because the vinegar may harm your vegetable plants as well.

Most household vinegar is 5% acetic acid. If you need something stronger, you can buy a bottle of 20% acetic acid vinegar. It works in the same way as the household vinegar, but it is usually faster and more effective. Be careful about using this vinegar on certain types of stone or concrete, because it may cause stains.

Corn gluten (this is not the same gluten that affects people with celiac disease) can be used to stop the weeds from growing in the first place, because it prevents the weed's seeds from germinating. The only problem with corn gluten is that it could potentially prevent the germination of your vegetable seeds as well, so it should not be used in a garden where you are starting the vegetables from seeds.

A long-handled "winged weeder" is a tool that can be found at any hardware or gardening store, and it makes weeding much easier. The truth is that it is very difficult to prevent weeds from growing, and one of the best things that you can do is to weed frequently in order to stop the weeds while they are young. This tool has a metal head that is in the shape of a "V," and it can be dragged along the top surface of the garden to uproot small weeds that may be growing. If you use this tool several times a week in the beginning of the growing season, it can help to slow the growth of the weeds in the season.

CHAPTER 6
HERBS FOR EVERY POT

Herbs will grow very well in containers outdoors and mean you can grow them in an each to reach location, such as by the kitchen door, or they can be brought indoors or put in a greenhouse to protect them during cold or inclement weather.

Containers could stand on the floor, or there could be hanging baskets or planters attached to walls or fences, to keep herbs away from the prying hands of children and the curious household pets.

Although the initial cost is much higher than growing in the soil, long term maintenance tends to be lower as you are not battling weeds growing through the soil. Containers are a great way to make a herb garden whether you have limited space, a balcony, or even a full garden. Some of us are banned by our significant others from growing herbs in the flower beds and must use strategically placed containers!

It is possible to grow different types of herb in a single container, though you need to make sure that they have similar soil and sun needs. There is no point growing a herb that likes a moist soil with one that likes a dry soil as one or the other will suffer. It is best to use annual herbs when putting multiple plants in a single container as perennial herbs will grow too big and crowd out the smaller herbs. However, if you have rosemary or lavender in a container, you can always grow a trailing herb such as creeping thyme which will hang over the edge of the container and not compete for space with the larger plant.

Seeds can be planted directly into containers or you can plant seedlings or store-bought plants, depending on the size of the container. A good way of extending your growing season is to start your herb seeds off indoors and then transplant them outdoors to containers when they have grown to a reasonable size and the risk of frost has passed.

There are many different types of container on the market made from anything from stone to plastic to resin or metal. What you buy will depend on your budget, the size container you want and the style container you like in your garden.

Porous materials such as clay dry out much faster than those made of plastic or resin due to evaporation, which will influence the amount of watering you need to do.

All containers need drainage holes so that excess water can seep out of the container. If there are not sufficient drainage holes, then you need to create some. Most herbs will die back if their containers get waterlogged. Self-watering containers are a good idea if you are growing in a greenhouse, but when used outside, they fill up with rainwater and drown your plants.

The key to making your herbs happy in containers is to use a good quality soil mix. Adjust the soil mix based on what the herb you are growing requires, but generally a mixture of a third each of vermiculite or pearlite, good quality compost and peat moss provides an excellent growing medium. Fill the container with soil and then push it down gently without compacting it as it is easier for the herb to grow in looser soil. Do not use soil from your garden as this will contain pests, weed seeds and potentially diseases too.

Containers are completely reliant on you for water and food. Once the herbs are established, their leaves will act as an umbrella and direct rainwater away from the container, so you still need to water them when it rains. Water when required directly onto the soil rather than onto the leaves to prevent run-off and mold forming if the leaves get too damp.

Your herbs will need fertilizing regularly too, typically starting two weeks after planting mature plants and four weeks after planting seedlings or after seeds have germinated. After this time, the plants will have depleted the nutrients in the soil, and they will need replenishing. Use a liquid feed such as a tomato feed or a general-purpose vegetable feed. This will have plenty of nitrogen in it that your plants need to grow healthy leaves. Seaweed based feeds are ideal for containers because they are packed with micro-nutrients and plants love these fertilizers. Avoid any fertilizers that are higher in potassium (K) or phosphorus (P) as these will encourage the herbs to form flowers at which point the taste of the leaves can often diminish. Feed once a week during the growing season and no more than once a month during the dormant season.

To encourage leafy growth, cut or pinch off any flower heads that form. This forces the plant to direct its energy on producing more growth so it can produce more flowers. Many herbs produce attractive flowers which will look great as well as attract beneficial insects to your garden.

Feel free to put some flowers in the containers with your herbs for some extra color and interest. Nasturtiums, marigolds and pansies all look great in containers plus have edible parts. These can brighten up a container of otherwise drab green herbs.

Containers are a great way for you to start an herb garden. In a larger container you can easily grow several different types of herb, giving you a nice variety to use in your home. You can plant containers in amongst growing herbs in the garden or you can plant multiple containers and place them around your garden, so the herbs get their ideal growing conditions.

Chapter 7
Kitchen Herbs

Herbs are very versatile plants that can add exquisite flavor to your cooking, can be used in a multitude of beauty products, but also have healing properties to help your wellbeing. They are incredibly useful, but easy to grow, with many able to grow all year round in many areas.

Chives

These are a mild flavored plant belonging to the onion group. You will be using their grass liken stems and these are cur from March through to October. Chives do not retain their flavor when dried so the best method for having this herb in your kitchen over the winter is to grow a few pots of this herb indoors.

The easiest way to grow your own chives is to grow pot grown specimens in your chosen location during autumn or Spring.

They really do prefer a sunny location and damp moist soil. Plant them about 9 inches apart and divide every 3 to 4 years.

Chives can be used in soups, salads, omelets, cream cheeses, mashed potatoes, sauces, potato salad. A very versatile and relatively easy herb to grow.

Dill

Even without its culinary used dill would be an attractive plant to have in your garden. It grows up to 2 feet tall with saucer size yellow flowers in July sitting atop a very attractive leathery foliage.

Dill responds very well to drying and its leaves retain their very distinctive flavor. The seeds provide an even stronger taste when lightly crushed.

Dill is easy to grow from seed, but the plant does not like being moved once it becomes established. With this in mind be sure to choose a location for your plant that is likely to be its home for a few years.

Choose a location that is sunny and well drained. Sow from seed in April and thin to about 12 inches apart when seedlings are firmly established. In prolonged spells of dry weather Dill plants need to be watered. Apply the water only to the base in order to be more economic with your water.

If you want to use Dill leaves for immediate use or for drying it is best to use young leaves.

Dill seeds are used in fish and rice dishes as well as being added to breads and cakes. Dill seeds are the most commonly used seeds for pickling cucumbers.

Lemon Thyme, Common Thyme, Caraway Thyme:

You have three varieties to pick from. Common thyme has the strongest flavor. Lemon thyme has a distinct citrus flavor and caraway has a caraway/pine type.

These are a tidy low growing evergreen shrub and are very aromatic. Because this plant is evergreen there is no need for drying, you have it all year round.

Choose a sunny, well drained location and plant pot grown thyme about 12 inches apart. Plant in early spring if the weather is fine. Lift and divide your Thyme plants every 3 years.

Common thyme needs to use sparingly and is most often associated with parsley when used in stuffing poultry dishes. However, it is also used as a rub for roasting and fish dishes as well as stews and soups.

Lemon thyme is particularly niche when used is custards and caraway thyme is useful for occasions when a slight one type flavoring is required.

Marjoram and Oregano:

The plant species Organum has many varieties; the majority are referred to a Marjoram but one in particular is referred to as oregano.

The type of Marjoram most commonly grown for culinary purposes is Sweet Marjoram. It can be grown from either seed or pot grown specimens. It is half-hardy so will die back at first Autumn frosts.

If growing from seed they will need to be sown under glass 1 March and then transferred to a sunny location at the end of May. You will need to leave about 9 inches between each plant.

Marjoram main culinary uses are for sprinkling on poultry or meat before roasting as well as for use in soups, rissoles and stuffing.

Rosemary:

This is actually evergreen but can be tender depending on your local weather conditions This shrub prefers a sunny and sheltered location with free draining soil.

It is ideal for a large container at the base of a south facing wall or for growing in a shrub border. To keep it compact and neat it needs regular picking and a good pruning every spring This pruning and picking should keep it at about 2 feet tall.

They can be grown from seed sown in May but the most sure-proof growing method is to plant pot-grown specimens.

Sage:

A very attractive shrub with grey-green and blue spike like flowers that could be grown just for its attractive appearance alone.

One plant should meet all your requirements so plant a pot grown specimen in a sunny and well drained location in spring.

After your Sage has flowered in late June/early July it will need to be lightly pruned.

Tarragon:

There are two types of Tarragon, French and Russian. You need the French variety as the Russian version has practically no taste.

Tarragon grows best in a well-drained soil in a sheltered situation. This herb is not completely hardy so if your locality is prone to severe frosts or biting winds it is always a good idea to cover the plant with straw or ashes in autumn. One plant should suffice as it is a very vigorous grower and will soon spread all over. If you want to restrict its growth you can grow it in a container.

Mint:

Mint is possibly the easiest of all the herbs to grow. It grows well is practically any soil in any weather conditions. In fact, it grows so well that some people struggle to contain its growth. For this reason, it is very often grown in containers to restrict the spread of its roots.

Spearmint (garden mint) and Bowles mint are the two most commonly planted types of mint. Round leaved mint and Bowles mint are the types most favored for making mint sauce.

Planting mint could not be easier. Just plant a couple of pieces of mint root about 2 inches deep and keep planting about 9 inches apart, in Autumn or early spring. If growing in containers you will need to provide a top dressing of mulch or compost in autumn. Other than its use in mint sauce and mint jelly it is also added to the water when boiling potatoes and peas.

Parsley:

It is easy to get confused with all the different varieties of Parsley. Simply put, if you want decorative Parsley choose the curly leaved variety, if you want greater flavor, choose the plain leaved variety.

Sowing parsley requires very fertile soil in semi-shade. Sow your seed in April to get a summer and autumn crop. Sow seed in august to get a winter crop.

Sow the seed ½ inch deep in fine soil but be prepared to wait. Germination takes a long time for Parsley. When seedlings appear thin them out to about 9 inches apart. In very dry weather it is important to keep them well watered.

To ensure a regular supply of fresh leaves you will need to pick regularly. Remove all flowering stems as they appear, however if you want your parsley to self-seed you can choose to leave some o the flowering stems on the plant in the second season.

Herbs for A Windowsill

Basil:

Basil is a tender plant that simply will not survive frost. It can be sown under glass in peat during March and April. It can then be planted out in early June to a reasonably fertile, well drained, sunny location.

When planting out keep the young plants about 12 inches apart. In order to produce a strong bushy plant, it is best to pinch out the growing tips regularly. Regular picking ensures fresh new leaf growth for further picking.

Basil is best preserved by using the ice-cube method rather than drying which almost totally destroys the flavor.

If you want Basil for winter you could left some of your Basil plants and place them in pots. These pots could be kept on the kitchen windowsill.

Basil is very widely used in cooking and is best known for its use with a huge number of Italian recipes however, it is also used for adding to minced beef, sausages, soups and salads.

Herbs for Heavy Soil

Fennel: Fennel can grow to be a huge plant, very often up to 5 feet tall. Because of this it is usually grown in an herbaceous border. It requires a sunny and well drained location

This perennial plant produces blue-green feathery foliage with yellow flowers. It is often confused with Dill which is shorter and less heavily flavored.

It can be grown from seed, but the easiest option is to grow it from a pot-grown specimen. Pick the leaves as you need them. The seeds can be harvested by waiting for the flower – heads to turn brown. Then secure a paper bag over each flower head. Now cut the stems and hang upside down in bunches. This technique is the same as used for harvesting Dill seeds.

The chopped foliage of fennel is used for soups, salads, fish and vegetable dishes. The seeds are often used when cooking oily fishes such as mackerel.

Herbs for Sandy Soil

Lemon verbena – summer only:

This is a tender shrub with very specific needs. It needs a sunny location with well-drained soil. However, it also needs some shelter. It can grow up to 10 feet tall with highly aromatic leaves. Depending on your locality it might also need protection from heavy frosts during winter.

Because of the potential size and their very aromatic leaves they are ideal for large pots at the base of a south facing wall. They can be trained against a trellis behind the pot to make a very impressive specimen pot plant. You won't need many of these, one or two will easily suffice.

Because of their intense aroma their use in very much a matter of personal taste. It's just trial and error, until you find an amount – that suits your palate. They make excellent potpourri so pick their leaves for drying when the falloff the plant in autumn.

Lemon Verbena is most commonly used in salads and desserts. Lemon and Mint Tea is claimed by many to be the most refreshing of all.

Coriander: Coriander should be grown directly into its permanent growing position. It likes well-drained, slightly lime soil in full sun. Sow directly into the soil in autumn or spring. Coriander self-seeds freely so expect a few new plants within a year or two. It will grow to about 2 feet tall with a very strong aroma.

Its leaves are used in a variety of dishes and are especially useful for curries, lentils, beans, onions, potatoes and chilies. Asian, Middle Eastern and Indian dishes use a lot of coriander.

Its young leaves and shoots can be used at any time. Its seeds are dried, roasted and ground prior to use.

Chapter 8
Benefits of Growing Plants in Container

There are various reasons why a lot of people start their own container garden. They are pretty easy to manage, and they are very convenient. You can always bring them with you, especially if you frequently move, they can serve as accents to the different rooms in your house, they are space-efficient, and they are very cost-effective. Here are some more of the benefits that container gardening has to offer.

Soil can be adjusted according to plants' requirements.

If you live in a place where the quality of soil is poor, it might be impossible to successfully grow and harvest plants, but with container gardening, you can easily buy soil or create a soil mix that your plant will fruitfully grow in. In addition, if the plants you wish to plant have different soil requirements, then you can simply place them in different containers and fill the containers with the correct soil types.

Weeding will be much easier. Because your plants are enclosed and contained in containers, weeding will be much easier and not much work.

Confines wild-growing plants. When wild-growing plants are freely planted in a garden, they can sometimes cause problems, as they tend to overtake other plants and grow in different places. With container gardening, however, this is not a problem, as the containers are able to enclose and contain the plant. If the plants grow too big for their containers, you can decide to transfer the plants and submerge them in your garden without removing them from their containers.

Protects plants from wild animals. If there are wild animals in the place where you live, plants planted in your garden might get destroyed or eaten. To avoid this, you can start an indoor garden instead.

Watering will be easier. Different plants have different water requirements. If you plant to grow various plants, watering will be much easier because you can simply water them individually without the hassle.

Bringing them with you is easy. If you frequently move to a new house or travel, container gardening is very ideal. Since they are in containers, you can effortlessly bring them with you without putting pressure on them and without stressing them out.

Moving them around will be effortless. Just like water requirements, different plants have different sunlight requirements too. One of the best things about growing plants in container gardens is that you can easily move them around your house to make sure that they get the right amount of sunlight that they need. If it's winter season, you can follow the sun and place them in an area where the sun shines best, or if it's summer season and the sun get too hot, you can relocate them to a place where there is partial shade.

The Disadvantages of Container Gardening

There are a limited number of disadvantages to container gardening. Some of them are as follows:

Limited space. Since plants are in a confined container, their growing space is confined as well.

Better for small plants. Container gardening is ideal for small plants. Usually, plants which are commonly grown out of containers, are edible ones like herbs.

Frequent watering. Although watering will be much easier if you have a container garden, you will find yourself watering more often. The reason is because the soil, as well as the moisture, are restricted to the dimensions of your containers.

Frequent fertilizing. Frequent watering can wash away the plants' essential nutrients from the soil. Therefore, you might need to fertilize more often than you normally would if they were planted in the ground.

Chapter 9
Container Plant Design

If you're an expert craftsman or you're even more a paint-by-numbers sort of individual, this part has something for you. Comprehension a touch about color hypothesis and how plant shapes and structures interrelate can mean the distinction between a ho-murmur container planting and one that stops activity.

In this part, you find plans and impulse for planning your own grower, idiot proof container combos, and thoughts for spreading your wings, container gardening-wise.

Making Beautiful Container Gardens

Ever recognize how well a few things go together? Like peanuts and baseball, crusty fruit-filled treat and dessert, stripes and plaids. This guideline applies to the container plant planet as well. A pot full of purple pansies might astonish the eye. However, watch what happens when you include a sprinkle of fragrant white hyacinths.

Blended plantings can run from unassuming to glorious. A hanging bushel consolidating petunias and verbena is pretty. A stately urn with an evergreen Alberta spruce stressed with tufts of two-toned, fragrant sweet William and encompassed by pale pink, trailing ivy geraniums can catch the attention of passersby almost instantly. An aggregation of cobalt blue, oversized grower showing a soil grown foods laden midget peach tree, a blooming mandevilla vine climbing a container-mounted trellis, and pots of bursting orange and red New Zealand impatiens can be eye-catching like nothing else.

Past acquainting you with the magnificent universe of blended plantings, this part gives you a nitty gritty guide to processing your own exceptional showcases. We blanket outline thoughts and familiarize you with the color wheel and how to consolidate colors successfully in a mixed bag of ways. We take a gander at other plan nuts and bolts, too — structure, composition, and extent — and demonstrate to you best practices to execute these plans into practically any beautiful plan.

Assuming that you're new to gardening, the methodology of picking plants might be moving, so we additionally give some container arrangement "formulas" in the part. As their culinary cousins, these formulas might be tweaked to incorporate top choice plants or to substitute plants that aren't accessible.

Enclosure Style

Looking around at the innumerable plants and containers that are accessible to you might be overwhelming. Where do you start? The first step is to decipher your arrangement style.

It is beneficial for you to think about the following –

Are you attracted to blowsy cabin enclosures where plants are packed together in a casual, apparently aimless way? Additionally, are you inclined towards clean hills of distinct plants differentiated by brightening mulch?

Do you like plants that develop thusly and that, or ones that are symmetrical?

What shades do your house, furniture, and wardrobes are in? Do you like brash and striking, unobtrusive and anything that falls in this category?

Do you like unusual things like small designs that carry a grin or utilize things for an unintended reason? Then you may portray your gardening style in that manner.

Addressing these inquiries can help you begin on your blended container plantings. In the event that you're anxious about your configuration abilities, begin with something safe. Then again go ahead despite any potential risks. When it's all said and done, you can dependably replant. There are two approaches to make blended plantings. One is to utilize one plant for every container and put different containers in a visually interesting manner. The different is to blend plants in a solitary container. By developing an assortment of plants, you can be certain to have an eye-catching ensemble for the duration of the season.

Plan Elements

You can play with the essential components of configuration like shape, composition, and the extent, and utilize them to add extraordinary profundity and investment to your blended plantings. Shape alludes to essential plant shape.

Upright, spiky iris, for instance, unmistakably has a contrasting shape to the round-leafed, falling ivy geranium. Composition is resolved by the look and feel of a plant's foliage and blooms and runs the array from barbarous and hard cactus to light and fancy greeneries. Both shape and surface are best when the components balance one another without seeking consideration.

No configuration examination is finished without a statement on the extent or scale. This is a crucial factor in the following two ways. The plants ought to be in the extent to the container, and the container and plant together might as well fit the area. Determining that everything fits together is as a rule a matter of parity.

A modest trailing plant in a colossal tub or a wide bush in a slender box basically doesn't work. Similarly, an enormous leafed perpetual plant looks odd on a minor table. Uniqueness is acceptable. However, it is important to determine if the jump isn't too extraordinary. Provided that you're indeterminate, you must try out potential fusions when you're shopping at the nursery.

Assemble plants and pots and see if the combo fits well for you. At that point envision it on your target location. Will it fill the space without disturbing it? These tips on shape, surface, and extent apply to your blended plantings:

Ensure beyond any doubt that the plant fits the pot. An outline normally looks best if little plants are utilized for minor pots as a part of little spaces, and bigger plants are held for substantial pots in huge spaces. Think about every plant's development estimate as a top priority when matching plant to pot, particularly with regards to trees and bushes. In spite of the fact that you can attach prune plants to help control their size, its best to utilize a container that can suit the plant's projected full-grown size.

Catch the eye and include adjustments with differentiating structures. Join spiky iris with adjusted geraniums, for instance. However, be mindful so as not to try too hard.

Create both a delicate and satisfying feel with finely textured, fancy plants. Lobelia, modest greeneries, and small flowery fillers are a couple of plants that possess all the necessary qualities. Fragile looking plants mollify hard container edges and mix well with different surfaces.

For a strong center, attempt enormous blossoms (zinnia or dahlia) or extensive, memorable leaves (hosta or elephant ear). These are especially adequate in substantial pots, which may be placed near a modest plant.

Group similar plants, yet don't hesitate to select plants with varying tallness. Evade extremes like tall bushes and trees coupled with ground hugging creepers

Use offset and scale for container situation, as well. A colossal barrel on a small yard gazes as out of spot as a minor dish plant lost on a broad deck.

A characteristic, progressive stream comes about because of tall plants when put around the container with moderate estimated plants in the middle and low or trailing ones along the edges. Decide the configuration cleverly, picking a mix of three separate sorts is a great place to begin if you're planting all annuals or a mix of diverse sorts of annuals, perennials, and woody plants.

Including Color

Numerous individuals think about the most obvious outline component to be a color, which likewise happens to the most enjoyable to play with. Take a gander at a color wheel and look at how it functions. Essential colors like red, blue, and yellow are equidistant on the wheel, and all different shades come about because of blending these three colors. Next, you have to find corresponding color inverse of these, which are yellow and violet or red and green, for instance. At last, you see symphonious colors mixing steadily between two essential shades, for example, red to orange to yellow. Shades allude to lighter and darker varieties of the same shade. In order to make you understand the fundamentals right away, here is a speedy first stage on what happens when you try different things with different mixtures:

For strong, vibrant looks, pick reciprocal colors (on inverse sides of the color wheel, for example, yellow and violet.

For more inconspicuous syntheses, pick amicable mixes of identified colors like blue, violet, and purple.

Create a relieving style with varieties or shades of the same color — pale pink to rose-red, for instance.

Add more than enough energy with stimulating hot colors utilizing red, orange, or yellow.

Cool things down with reviving soul, greens, and violets.

Don't disregard white. It includes welcome extent, lightens dim ranges, and works with all different shades.

Consider foliage, as well. Notwithstanding each shade of green possible, leaf colors incorporate gleaming ash, yellow, chartreuse, profound maroon, splendid red, and variegated (multi-toned).

Recollect that both plants and the container can help the color plan. A sparkling, shining blue earthenware pot will set a much distinctive tone than a matte, terra-cotta one. Exemplary shade plans are one thing, and individual taste is the other. The primary concern is to pick colors that you like. If you like them, they can't be wrong. If you're striving for a rainbow impact, consider planting orange marigolds and pink petunias, or organizing a basic, single-color presentation.

Consistency and Compatibility

As an exceptional marriage, a great container planting comprises of perfect parts that complement each other well. Hence, the plants and the container must be complementing by nature. Provided that you're planting more than one sort of plant in a container, verify the plants have comparable prerequisites for sun/shade and soil dampness. Rosemary and thyme are great sidekicks because both like full sun and decently emptied soils. However, rosemary and coleus are not all that great together.

Chapter 10
Best Plant to Grow in Containers

Plant your veggie container greens at the similar time you will plant around the patch. Depending upon what kinds of veggies you wish to produce, you could start kernels in your planters, grow uproots from stones started inside, or buy transplants from a patch center.

Start your vegetable planter garden harvests from pits sown straight in the pot. Regardless of whether you are implanting seeds or uproots, thoroughly dampen the pot before you lodge. Soak the potting amalgam completely and allow it to rest for a limited number of hours to exhaust excess liquid.

Plant germs according to the set directions and because not the entire seeds would germinate, embed more than you demand, then attenuate the spare later. Set uproots at the identical level they were budding in their planter. This is an exception for tomatoes, which you could detach the lower foliage and embed them profounder in the pot.

After rooting, water mildly, but comprehensively to settle down the spores or uproots. Keep the earth in your veggie container rockery from sunstroke as quickly by covering it with leaf mold, straw or compost.

The top five vegetables suitable for container gardening are:

Tomatoes - Transplant a plant for every five-gallon container. Recommended diversities are Early Girl, Patio Princess, Pixie, Super Bush, Tumbling Tom and Vilma.

Pepper – Make two transplants in a five-gallon container using recommended varieties like Gypsy, Long Red Cayenne or New Ace.

Eggplant – Plant one in a five-gallon container from recommended varieties, such as Black Beauty, Orlando and Patio Mohican.

Broccoli – Make one transplant in a five-gallon container using any of the recommended varieties consisting of DeCicco, Green Comet or Small Miracle.

Carrots - Direct pip into a five-gallon deep planter, thinning to three inches separately. Recommended variations include Danver's Half Long, Little Finger, Short 'n' Sweet and Thumbelina

Anybody, on any stage of horticultural experience, could indulge a desire for delightful, high-quality produces by mounting fruits in planters. It demands a negligible investment of money and time yet rewards luscious bonuses. Though highly any fruit can be developed in a pot, there are time-tested pets to start with as they simply adapt to holding their cores confined. Gardening in planters though can be additionally labor-intensive as compared with growing matching plants inside the terrain.

The top five fruits suitable for container gardening are:

Mulberry Tree

Unlike its comparable sounding networks, the strawberry or blueberry, the mulberry is a sapling. If you begin one from a seed, it can be at least 10 years before you get a fruit, making it not exactly exciting. Accelerate the course by buying an organically raised semi-dwarf variation from your nearby nursery.

Place it inside a huge pot either outside in sufficient sunshine, or inside in a temperate, bright room. The mulberry creates large, extended, black berry similar in appearance to a three inches long blackberry. The crop usually matures in the beginning of summer.

Strawberries

Strawberries are a very popular pod for family gardening for the reason that they yield fruits exceptionally quickly, besides requiring a comparatively small expanse. Strawberries make certain an exceedingly high vitamin C substance and are finely suited to freeze up and meting out jams.

Fig Tree

Reader's Digest had stated that all variability of fig ripens more severely if their cores are narrowed to a big pot, yet Negro Largo accomplishes particularly glowing as an indoor plant. The added great craze about it is that it favors indirect sunshine, making it perfect for studios which do not get much direct sunlight.

Pineapple

There is a way to grow delicious, sugary pineapple by the side of a house. Actually, no more than it is possible, it is pretty easy. As said by the Tropical Permaculture, the pineapple is among the small number of tropical capsules which are truly well suitable to developing in planters.

Peaches

Natural or else genetically dwarf assortments like bonanza can be cultivated as petite standards on 75 centimeters or 30 inches stems. Keep them within the home in a well-lighted, sunny location in heats averaging 53°F or 12°C until the drupe sets, and then they would require upper temperatures of an average of 68°F or 20°C. You need to ventilate them spontaneously in hot weather though.

CHAPTER 11
REQUIREMENTS FOR GROWING A SUCCESSFUL CONTAINER GARDEN

The following tips can be used by beginners to help them on their way to successfully growing vegetables in containers:

1. **Don't go too small or too few on the drainage holes.**

Proper drainage is one of the most important aspects of growing vegetables in containers. Without proper drainage, water will pool at the bottom of your container. This can result in the roots of your plants rotting away and it can promote the growth of fungi that cause damping off and all sorts of other problems.

Make sure you have enough drain holes in the bottom of your containers to let pooled up water drain out. Too few or too small of drain holes will leave you with saturated soil.

2. **Well-fed plants are happy plants that will grow big and strong.**

Don't underestimate the nutrients your plants need to grow big and strong. Watering your plants removes nutrients from the soil and your plants use up nutrients as they grow. Most potting soils start off devoid of nutrients and get worse as time progresses. It's up to you to make sure the correct nutrients are added.

Start your plants in nutrient-rich soil and regularly feed them with compost or fertilizer designed to restore the nutrients that are being removed. Your best bet is to use a combination of slow-release fertilizer and liquid fertilizer. Mix the slow release fertilizer into your soil before you add it to the container and then supplement the soil with liquid fertilizer once every couple of weeks.

3. Choose the plants you combine in a container wisely.

Some plants are better neighbors than others. Placing a plant that requires a heavy nutrient load in the same container with a fragile plant that doesn't do well when forced to compete for nutrients will more often than not result in the bigger, stronger plant crowding out its weaker neighbor.

Pay close attention to the watering, soil and sunlight needs of the plants you're thinking about planting together. You want them to be as close as possible. Planting a plant that requires full sunlight in a container with a plant that prefers only a few hours of sunshine a day will mean one of your plants isn't going to get the amount of sunlight it prefers. There's an abundance of information out there regarding specific plants and their needs and it would serve you well to do a bit of research before combining plants in containers.

4. Save the seed packet.

You should always keep the seed packet your seeds came from. They provide you with the information you need to ensure your plants grow big and strong. If there are any questions later on down the road, you're going to really wish you had the seed packet.

It also comes in handy when it comes time to reorder seeds for the next year. If you had a good growing experience and liked the vegetables you got, you'll know which seeds to reorder. If your experience was bad, you'll know which seeds to avoid the next time around.

5. Don't overreact, but don't wait until it's too late.

When problems crop up in the garden people tend to go to one extreme or the other. They'll either sit on their hands and wait, hoping for the best or they'll pull the sick plants immediately in hopes of stopping the problem dead in its tracks. While these reactions may be appropriate in some situations, it's a bad idea to react this way without understanding why you're taking the action you're taking.

Diseases and pest attacks happen for a reason.

If a plant starts dying or looking sick, it's important to identify exactly what's wrong, along with what could have caused it. Pulling your plants and starting over isn't effective because the results will likely be same the next time around if changes aren't made. Trying to wait a problem out isn't going to work unless you're sure your plants are healthy and able to survive.

Determine what's wrong and take decisive action to keep the problem from getting worse. Keep your reaction appropriate to the situation at hand. It's rarely a good idea to take things to either extreme. The answer usually lies somewhere in the middle.

6. Choose the right size container for your plants.

Make sure you carefully consider the size the plants you're planting will grow to when you're choosing the container, you're going to plant them in. Trying to grow a large plant in a small or unstable container can be an exercise in frustration.

When I was first starting out, I planted an artichoke plant in a small bucket I had lying around. I'd never seen a full-grown artichoke plant and severely underestimated how big it would be when full-grown. It grew nicely and sprouted a couple stalks. They grew and grew and then grew some more. The plant became top-heavy and the slightest breeze would send the bucket toppling over. I lost one entire stalk and a couple buds off of another stalk before I wised up and braced the container.

Had I of picked the right container to start with, I would have been able to harvest at least 7 more artichokes than I ended up with. I learned my lesson and now I always overestimate the size of the container I'm going to need. If the container ends up being too big, I know the next time around that I can use a smaller container.

7. Get good quality seeds and seedlings.

Buy plants and seeds from quality sources.

If you buy the cheapest seeds and seedlings you can find, you're going to get what you pay for. Spend a little more for quality seeds and you'll find you have more plants that sprout and mature into strong, healthy plants. If you're buying your plants from a big box retailer, don't buy plants that look like they've been sitting around for a while. It's no fun to buy a plant only to find it's already root bound.

8. Don't go too light on the water

Make sure you're giving your plants enough water.

When you're watering your plants from the top, the natural inclination is to go with what you see and to stop watering once the top of the soil appears properly watered. When you stop at this point, only the top gets water. The soil a few inches down will still be dry. Since a plant's roots are usually at least 4 to 5 inches below the soil, your plants aren't going to get the water they need.

Instead of watering until the topsoil appears to have enough moisture, water until you see water start to trickle out of the drainage holes. This means the water has made it all the way down through the soil and all of the soil in the container is wet.

9. Don't plant too soon or too late.

You need to plant your seeds at the right time. Plant too early in the season and your plants will either freeze to death or they'll be stunted and week. Some plants won't flower if they're planted too early in the season. Plant your vegetables too late in the season and you won't be able to harvest them before the weather turns bad and destroys your crops.

Follow manufacturer's instructions and keep a close eye on the weather reports in your area. A late-season frost or early storm can be avoided by moving your plants indoors until it's passed.

9. Enjoy yourself.

Every once in a while, I meet a gardener who's a complete mess. They've worked themselves into a frenzy worrying about anything and everything that could happen to their plants. Gardening is hard work, and there are things that can and do happen to crops, but it's supposed to be fun and rewarding. If you aren't enjoying it, you might as well forget about gardening and buy your vegetables from the store.

Chapter 12
The Right Potting Soil Mix For Your Plant

The type of soil you use in your container will vary depending upon what plants you are growing. Blueberries like a more acidic soil whereas tomatoes like free draining soil. Basil likes slightly more moist soil. I will talk about what I consider the best general-purpose soil mix for your containers but if you are growing plants with specific soil requirements then you will need to adjust this appropriately.

You can buy general purpose potting mixes from stores which will do the job, and most are adequate. The main issue with these tends to be that they do not drain very well, and you end up with very soggy soil after heavy rain.

I tend to mix up a large trash can full of potting mix and then I will adjust it as necessary according to the plants I am potting. It does work out quite cheap, but it also makes sure the plants thrive and do well.

If you can avoid it you do not want a heavy potting mix because it will make the pot very heavy if you want to move it. A loose and porous soil will be more efficient at transporting food, water and air to the roots of your plants.

You may be tempted to use soil out of your garden in your pots, but I would strongly advise against it. This soil isn't clean or sterile and it is going to be full of seeds as well as possible pests and disease. If you use garden soil then your pot will be sprouting weeds faster than your plants can grow so avoid using this. It is must better to make your own soil mix as it will be sterile and not contain weed seeds.

You can see in this pot a baby gooseberry busy which was planted in soil taken from the allotment as the plant needed rescuing, but it has grown a lot of weeds in just a few days.

The pest soil mix, in my opinion, is a mixture of a third each of peat moss, compost and perlite (or vermiculite). You can add some horticultural sand which will help with drainage if necessary. Ideally the compost should come from multiple sources, but this may not be practical in all cases.

For most plants this is going to be more than adequate but for plants that need free draining soil such as lavender, succulents and cacti then you will need to add extra sand. Some plants such as primrose prefer moist soil in which case increase the amount of peat moss to help with water retention.

Building on the basic container mix, this mixture works well and has a few additional benefits too:

- 1 bucket peat moss
- 1 bucket perlite or vermiculite
- ½ bucket compost
- 2 cups horticultural sand
- 2 cups time release fertilizer pellets
- ½ cup lime (offsets the acidity of the peat to keep the pH neutral)

Mix this up well and you will have a great potting mix that is very beneficial for your plants. A bucket will contain about 2½ gallons. Using the above quantities, you will have enough to fill around five 12" hanging baskets or two 14" tubs.

Typically, potting mix is sold in quarts whilst pots are sold by their diameter which can make it hard for you to work out how much soil you need. To give you an idea the following shows you roughly how much soil you need for each pot size.

Pot Size (inches)	Soil Amount (quarts)
8	3
10	6
12	8
14	12
16	20
20	24
24	28
30	72
36	96

For hanging baskets this is slightly different due to their shape:

Basket Size (inches)	Soil Amount (quarts)
12	6
16	10

Window boxes are different again:

Basket Size (inches)	Soil Amount (quarts)
24x6	12
36x6	20

This will give you a good idea of how much soil you need for different sized containers which will help you to minimize waste. At the end of the day you need to adjust the soil mix according to your choice of plants and their needs, but the soil mixes detailed above are a great starting point which your plants will love.

Chapter 13
Plants for Year-Round Container

There are things to consider when choosing year-round plants for containers. Pot's size, type, material, and the condition of the environment to place containers, are the things to consider. Also think about what it will take to care and maintain the plants all year round. The attention you need to give to your garden varies depending on your purpose of gardening - whether for growing edibles or for beautification or both. However, the primary consideration here is whether you would choose to grow annual plants to provide year-round crops or perennial plants. Choosing perennial plants will not only provide bounty edibles throughout the year but also require lesser effort. Here are some plants that are great for year-round containers:

Fruit trees

Fruit trees are great for year-round containers. Consider plants like a dwarf apple or citrus trees, cherries, apricots, plums, and other popular fruit trees. They all look great and produce maximum yields all year round. They will flourish through the seasons all year, and their buds will give your garden a very pleasant visual appeal. Examples of fruit trees for containers include; Cherries, Peaches, Apples, Lemons, Figs, Tangerines, Limes, etc.

Perennial Vegetables

Perennial Vegetables are also great for year-round containers. These plants maintain a healthy look all year round. Apart from the lovely visual display they exhibit, they also produce good yield all year round. Examples of perennial vegetables to grow in containers include; Blueberries, Asparagus, Artichokes, Raspberries, Lovage, Watercress, etc. Vegetables like Kale, Garlic, and Radicchio are perennial but are usually grown as annuals.

Perennial Herbs

Perennial herbs will thrive all year round as well. From their edible produce, you get to harvest useful culinary herbs throughout year. They provide you with continuous harvest for your kitchen. Some of the perennial herbs you can try are; Mint, Lavender, Greek Oregano, thyme, sage, chives, mint, rosemary, etc. They also give your garden an excellent visual display.

Perennial Flowers

Different flowers bloom at different seasons of the year. An idea to create a fantastic flowering garden all year round is to grow flowers that bloom at different seasons together in your garden. Perennial flowers thrive all year round, and by growing different varieties together, you keep your garden attractive all through the year. Plants in this category include; Salvia, Hydrangea, Hellebores, Hosta, Aster, Daylily, etc.

Other plants for year-round containers are yucca, boxwood, Pieris, Arborvitae, Bergenia, Variegated red-twig dogwood, Heucheras, and Fulda glut. They are beautiful, colorful, and shine radiantly in containers. Another way that you can enjoy year-round planting is by adding the idea of the polytunnel to your container garden. This can be of huge advantage if rightly done. It will enable you to grow plants and harvest them even when they are out of season or even when they would typically not do well at that particular season of the year. Purchase a good polytunnel that matches the available space in your garden but, at the same time, be conscious of how it will affect other things in your garden, such as when rain falls, whether the polytunnel will hinder drainage. Polytunnel looks almost like a greenhouse, but not the same. If you intend to get a polytunnel for your garden space, ensure there is enough ventilation in it and get an irrigation kits for an effective watering system for the containers in it.

Chapter 14
Tips for Watering Container Plants

Watering needs are extremely important for any kind of plant whether you are growing vegetables, fruits, flowers, or just ornamental houseplants. However, when it comes to container gardening, water is another factor that needs special consideration and planning in order for your plants to survive and thrive. Since containers don't have the natural drainage system your plants would have if planted in the ground, figuring out the water amount and frequency is vital to their growth. You don't want to over-water or under-water – both have disastrous consequences for a container garden. The water your plants need can vary significantly according to location (indoors or outdoors), environment (weather and temperature), and specific plant requirements.

Location – Whether your plants are in a controlled location (indoors) or exposed to seasonal temperatures (outdoors) will determine how often they need to be watered. In general, container plants growing outside will usually require daily watering and sometimes twice daily during hot weather seasons. Plants outside are more vulnerable to death by under-watering while plants indoors can easily be over-watered and drown.

Environment – If your container garden is outside and exposed to the elements, most likely it will require extra water during the hottest parts of the year. While heat can help the plants grow faster, it also dries out the soil faster making daily watering essential. The hotter weather can also be a bigger issue for plants indoors if you don't have an air conditioner and controlled temperature setting inside. Windy weather outside can also dry soil faster, so if you live in an area that usually deals with a lot of wind, you need to monitor the water needs of your plants closely.

Plant Requirements – How much water a plant needs also depends on it optimal growing needs. Some plants grow better if they dry out completely between watering while others grow best if the soil is always damp. This characteristic varies from plant to plant, and you should be able to find the soil recommendation on the seed label or store packaging material…and of course, such specific information is easily found online just by searching for the best growing environment for whatever plants you're trying to grow.

Self-Watering & Vacation-Watering Methods

While container gardening is indeed a relatively easy way to grow plants and edibles, water needs can be a bit challenging to meet if you are super busy or go on vacation while your plants are growing. But you don't have to let watering stop you from enjoying time away from home because there are some inexpensive ways you can provide adequate water to your plants without having to water them in person every day.

Water Bottle Method – You know those millions of empty plastic water and soda bottles that wind up in landfills and polluting the environment around the world? Well, you can use them to help yourself, your plants, and the planet all at the same time! Watering your plants with bottles is surprisingly simple but quite effective. All you have to do is place some small rocks in the bottom of the bottle (to stabilize it in case of wind gusts), poke some holes in it, fill with water, and place in the container right next to your plant. The water will slowly trickle out and provide your plant with the hydration it needs to both survive and thrive. You will need to do a little experimenting to see how many holes you need to poke in the bottle in order to determine how fast the water needs to drain out, but it is worth the effort. If you are going to be away from home for a few days, the bigger the bottle the better – even empty milk jugs can do the trick, and you will enjoy helping your plants and the environment at the same time.

Plastic Baggie Method – This method works similarly to the way the plastic bottle method works, and it is one more way to use items that would otherwise wind up in a landfill. Gently used zipper-type bags can be filled with water and placed on the soil next to your container plant. There needs to be at least 2-3 tiny holes in the plastic bag so water can leak out and hydrate your plant, and viola! You've got a self-watering plant. One benefit this method holds above the bottle method is baggies can be molded to fit in between plants in the same pot or can fit in other tight places where a bottle won't fit.

Clay Pot Method – Another ingenious trick to take some of the work out of watering your plants sufficiently is by using clay pots to provide that continuous moisture your plants need to survive. This method calls for unglazed clay pots that have their drainage holes sealed with clay, putty, or even duct tape. Simply bury the pot next to your plant so the rim of the pot is level with the soil surface in your container. Fill the pot with water that will gradually be absorbed as the soil dries out thus watering the plant without any additional

CHAPTER 15
CONTAINER MATERIAL

Be creative when picking pots for plants.

You can use any material for pot in as much as it does not get too hot under the sun and drains well. If your pots do not have sufficient drainage holes, ensure you make a few good-sized holes on them. If you cannot drill holes on a particular planter, it can be however worked around by planting in a different pot and situate it in your preferred container.

You also need to put the size of the plants you would be growing into consideration when choosing a pot. If you prefer a smaller container, the soil may not be able to obtain sufficient moisture, in no time plants will turn out to be root bound and dry out, hence leading to plant destruction. Then again, if your container is vast, your crops might use up all their energy on developing root and not sufficiently on growth. The West Virginia University Extension Service stated that shallow-rooted plants such as herbs, peppers, lettuce, and most annuals require a planter of no less than six-inch in diameter with eight-inch soil depth. Bigger containers such as ½ whiskey barrels and bushel basket are suitable for growing pole beans, cucumbers, tomatoes, and most perennial crops.

Planters and pots are available in many diverse shapes, sizes, and materials. Whichever type of container you choose, take the area where it would be utilized into consideration and plan accordingly. Select containers in appropriate quantity to the size of the plant.

Terra-Cotta

Terra-Cotta is available in different sizes and shapes. The pots look great with their plain color that brings out the beauty of nearly any plant. The product of porous soil rich in iron, it has breathing ability which keeps potting soils calm and drains surplus dampness out of the plant roots to maintain their health status. The significant issues with terra-cotta are that it can quickly dry out particularly in hot climate and quite fragile (can be easily broken). Some growers choose glazed terra-cotta pots as they obtain water a lot better.

Plastic

If you don't care about having plants that ultimately grow to cover their pots or the look of the container, plastic is a better option. Plastics pots hold moisture well, durable and are reasonably cheap. They are also not heavy, which makes reorganizing your gardens an easy task. If your container garden is situated in an extremely sunny area, you are advised not to use a dark colored or black plastic. As they quickly get hot and also absorb heat which can cause roots damage. Bright colored container reflects the warmth and maintains the coolness in the roots.

Wood

Wood is among the most original and handy containers for gardening. They look good, not heaving and hold water well. If you are to choose wood containers, ensure they are made out of wood that is resistant to rotting such as redwood or cedar and confirm the construction quality since wood will naturally expand and shrink in the elements. Containers made out of soft-wood or pine can be as well used but has to be painted with a harmless paint to avoid rot. Wooden containers can be easily made with some scrap wood and some creative idea without stress.

Concrete

Concrete is ideal for holding large plants that need more support to keep them healthy due to its heaviness. It possesses excellent insulating materials, protecting tender roots systems by maintaining a calm soil atmosphere. With a concrete container, you can leave your plants outdoor over the winter with no fear of harm (or even if you're planting in public area) since it has an additional advantage of preventing people from inadvertently working off with your valued pots or plants.

Essentially, the criteria that you use for the pots should be first about the functionality, second about the appearance, and only lastly about the cleverness or creativity that it depicts.

Begin choosing the largest vessels that you can find or afford as these will hold the most soil, retain the most water and nutrients, and ensure that your plants get the best possible conditions. They also end up being the best for "low maintenance" too.

Design

The design of your pots is really up to you. You can choose pots that have more than one part in them, in order to make a container garden that contains more than one herb, or you can have herbs in separate pots. If you are concerned about the color of the pots, be sure not to use a black pot since exposure to a lot of sunlight will heat up the roots too much and damage the plant. White and light-colored pots are best suited for sunny areas while black pots should be used in shaded areas to attract the warmth of the sun.

Choosing a pot for herbs is pretty easy! As long as it has good drainage, is in a decent size, and made of a material that's suitable, then it's all good.

Chapter 16
Container Sizes

When it comes to container gardening, the type and size of the container is going to matter greatly. The more soil you're able to give your plants, the better off they will be. But there are limitations to everything.

Generally, the largest container possible is going to be the best for your plants. Small ones tend to dry out quicker and need watering on a daily basis. Self-watering planters that are for urban balconies and patios will extend the time between watering.

The most important thing to think about is the depth of the container. Plants that have deep root systems are going to be stunted and unhealthy if they're not in the right amount of space. Remember, the deeper the pot, the larger the amount of moist soil there will be and the less often you're going to need to water. The exception to that rule is the self-watering planters. Here's a more in-depth guide to the size of your planter for specific plants.

Container Size

Of course, the larger, the better, but there are some guidelines as to what you can put into the smaller pots and what you might want to place in the larger pots.

Choosing a pot that's the right size for your plants is going to ensure that your container garden is a success. A pot that's too small equals a plant that's not going to produce as much, and you're going to need to work harder to keep them alive and growing. If the pot is too large, then you're going to spend more money on soil than is really necessary. Here's a guide to help you choose pots that are the right size for the right plant.

24" Diameter Pot

A twenty-four-inch pot is going to hold some of the following plants comfortably:

- Summer Squash
- Large Peppers
- Indeterminate Tomatoes
- Artichokes
- Cucumbers
- A Combination of Vegetables and Herbs

18" Diameter Pot

Eighteen diameter pots will hold some of the following plants comfortably:

- Eggplant
- Cauliflower
- Broccoli
- Cabbage
- Greens and Herbs
- Determinate Tomatoes
- Small Peppers

The right container for tall tomato plants is going to be at least two feet wide. Indeterminate tomato plants are going to need pots at least twenty-four inches wide. Be sure to choose a cage that will fit inside the pot.

14" Diameter Pot

Four-inch diameter pots will hold some of the following plants:

- Herbs
- Collards
- Cabbage
- Lettuce
- Spinach
- Arugula

10" Diameter Pot

A ten-inch diameter pot will hold the following:

- Strawberries
- Herbs
- Lettuce

You should remember that not all pots are going to be circular and high. Shallow-rooted plants like lettuce are going to be happy in a container bigger in diameter than it is tall. However, vegetable plants are going to need deeper pots. Broad plants, like pumpkin and zucchini, will like containers that are broad and deep. Half barrels are great for the bigger plants like squash and zucchini. Use your judgment and give your plants plenty of space for the best harvest. Sometimes experience is going to give you the best advice for the future.

Chapter 17
Where to Place Your Container

The beauty of container gardening is the fact you can take full advantage of whatever space you have. It doesn't matter where you live, you can find space for a few containers. Containers can be located on porches, stairs and decks. They can line walkways and sidewalks, and they can be used along fences that mark property lines. They can hang from eaves or climb trellises.

If you live in an apartment, they can be used on balconies, rooftop gardens or window boxes. You can also grow vegetables indoors in your kitchen and in sunny windows.

That being said, just what is needed to successfully grow vegetables in containers.

How Much Sun Do Vegetables Actually Need?

Plants produce their own food through a process of photosynthesis. They capture energy through the sun and convert it into a chemical energy that supports their growth. The more sun they receive, the more energy they can put into growing and producing foliage, fruit and seeds.

Southern exposure will give your plants the greatest light and heat possible. Western or Eastern exposures should be your second choice, while a Northern exposure produces the least amount of light and heat.

Follow the Sun

When deciding on the placement of your containers, keep an eye on the sun for a few days. Make a note of any buildings or trees and where the cast shadow lands during the day. It's not enough to have a southern exposure, but you should also be aware of shadows that might prevent your vegetables from getting the greatest amount of needed sunlight to produce the best results possible.

Wind should also be a consideration when planning the location of your garden. I've seen many a container be toppled over by the wind. I've also seen plants shredded by wind just at the peak of their fruiting season. If you have a wind tunnel or high winds going through your property, be sure to take this into consideration and place your containers in a protected spot away from windy areas.

Make Your Containers Movable

A large planted container can easily weigh 100 pounds or more. This will help you move garden containers if the location needs to be changed to take advantage of the movement of the sun or to protect the plants from wind, hail or thunderstorms. This will also be helpful in the fall if you want to move them into the garage or other sheltered area to protect them from an early frost.

Make Sure Water is Accessible

Another point that needs to be addressed when locating your container garden is the accessibility of water. Containers need lots of water and if you find yourself lugging buckets of water every day, you'll soon tire of this project and decide it's just not worth the effort.

Container gardens take a lot of water. A fully-grown tomato plant in a 5-gallon bucket takes a gallon a day. You may not need to spend a lot of time tilling and weeding but be aware that container gardens have to be watered on a regular basis. You can't wait until tomorrow, because you'd rather go to the beach today.

Water before you go, or you'll find that beautiful tomato plant wilted beyond repair if you ignore it too long. Even self-watering containers must be filled, so be sure to locate them near a source of water.

A very long hose that can be rolled onto a garden hose reel is ideal. As long as you are in the hose department, check out watering nozzles. There are many types of nozzles, so be sure to get one that provides a wide range of sprays needed for various purposes such as watering, misting, and fertilizing.

Chapter 18
Fertilizing Your Container

When grown in pots with limited space, plants are cut off from the rich source of nutrients that they would otherwise get if grown outdoors. At the same time, it is a fact that no matter how good the pot soil mixture was from the get-go, it will become sterile over time as essential nutrients are leached out and washed away through water leaking through the little holes in the bottom of the pots.

The gradual depletion of nutrients in the pot growing medium is the main cause of almost all the failures of novice container gardeners who do not have any knowledge of this. That's why fertilization plays such a vital role in container gardening.

So, to ensure a rich environment for their potted plants, gardeners have to make a point of intentionally adding nutrients via fertilizers.

However, fertilization can be a little bit complicated when you first begin gardening. As a gardener, you can't just dump some fertilizer into the containers and take it for granted that everything's done!

There are many facets that you need to take into account when it comes to feeding your potted plants – they encompass which kinds of fertilizer for different types of vegetation and how to practice this process of fertilization correctly.

There are many kinds of organic fertilizers used in container gardening. They all have their own pros and cons due to their different characteristics and effects.

There is no one best type in this case. You should make up your mind which ones to choose as the constant source of food for your plants depending on the specific needs of your garden.

There are some facts you should know about fertilizers to enable you to make an informed choice.

As a rule, the packaging of any kinds of fertilizers shows its content ingredient ratio via the three numbers printed with a fixed order. They represent the percentage by weight of the N-P-K, also known as Nitrogen, Phosphorous, and Potassium respectively.

Each of these elements has a different effect on the plants. In terms of the first figure in the trio - nitrogen- this nutrient boosts the growth of foliage, causing the plant to produce plenty of lush, green leaves. Nitrogen also fulfills the function of taking care of the overall health of the plants.

The second number indicates the amount of phosphorus contained in the fertilizer. Phosphorus is known to help the plant roots to develop well and to embed themselves firmly into the growing medium, improving the ability of plants to absorb nutrients easily.

The third and last number indicates the amount of potassium. This element helps the stem of plants to grow strong and healthy. It contributes to the plant having a good shape, color, and in the case of vegetables, taste.

There are many different kinds of fertilizers with different ratios of the three ingredients. Your task is to choose the right kinds based on the types of plants in you of your garden.

For leafy plants or vegetables such as lettuce, herbs, ferns, etc. you will need a fertilizer with a particularly high ratio of nitrogen. The other ingredients also help and are also necessary, but nitrogen will cause the plant to produce plenty of lush foliage.

However, when it comes to plants grown for their fruits or flowers, you need to watch out for this type of fertilizer. Too much nitrogen will leave your edibles such as cucumbers and tomatoes with too many leaves and small fruits and flowers. In this case, you should go for a fertilizer with a higher ratio of phosphorous, especially when the plants are supposed to set buds. They need stronger roots to take up more nutrients than usual in this difficult phase of producing flowers and fruit.

Plants grown for their underground root output such as carrots, beets and potatoes, need more potassium to develop the roots well into a large and delicious crop.

Fertilizing in the right way

Fertilizers can only be utilized by the plants when they are applied correctly. The instructions on their packaging should be read and followed. However, for the best chance of the great results, you may need a few more tips.

Fertilize before potting

You can apply the nutrient solution in advance by adding fertilizer to your potting mixture. Use slow-release fertilizers in the form of nutrients in pellets and mix them with the soil in the proportion stated on the packaging. It will take a while for this kind of fertilizer to take effect, but it is a really rewarding practice! Your soil can be filled with sufficient nutrients at root level for the new plants.

Do not fertilize when the soil is dry

You should use water to help the process of fertilization because water can speed up the absorption of nutrients from fertilizers via the soil into the plants. On the other hand, a lack of water can cause residue after use, which will result in the nutrients building in your pots and perhaps burning the plants.

Foliage feeding

Not only the roots, but also the leaves, can absorb a significant amount of nutrients. Therefore, to optimize the effects of fertilization, you can use a foliage nutrient solution that gets sprayed onto the leaves and gets absorbed through them.

There are many products for this application on the market, although they aren't as popular as conventional kinds of fertilizer that get mixed into the soil. Just be careful not to apply this type of fertilizer when you are expecting rain, as it will just get washed off the leaves. Also make sure you don't apply it when the plants are in direct sunshine, or the leaves may burn.

Daily fertilization

Generally, most gardeners will fertilize their plants at two-week intervals with water-soluble types of fertilizers. However, you can also make a weak nutrient solution to be used with everyday watering.

In this case, do not mix the fertilizers with the original ratio instructed on the packaging; you have to make a mixture with half the strength instead. After preparing, you can water the plants as usual.

Keep in mind to leave one day a week to use just plain water to prevent the threat of the salt buildup and an excess of nutrients.

Consider natural fertilizers

Besides the kinds of fertilizers available at the shops, you can also use some types of natural fertilizer such as compost, mulch, etc. now and then. These handmade fertilizers are very friendly to the environment and your plants because they leave no salt buildup or residue in the long term.

However, it takes a very long time for them to be broken down and take effect. During this lengthy process, your plant containers can become a great retreat for harmful insects and pests. Sometimes, they also give off nasty smells. To prevent this, make sure you rot the compost down well in the compost bucket before applying it to your plants. It should resemble dry, crumbly soil and should have a pleasant smell.

Chapter 19
Caring For Your Container Garden

There are a few simple, easy to follow maintenance steps you can take to keep your container garden looking its best throughout the growing seasons. They range from the tools and materials you will use, plant containers, water sources and scissors/pruners,

You should fertilize your plants regularly. Rapidly growing plants need a lot of nutrients. The need for fertilizing is imperative, considering the frequent watering and the limited amount of soil in container gardens. The mixing of slow release fertilizer into the potting soil is also an important measure in making sure they receive the right amount of nutrients.

A standard potting compost is usually peat or peat based. All plant fertilizes contain 3 key elements: Nitrogen (N), Phosphorus (P) and Potassium (K). The balance of these nutrients will vary from fertilizer to fertilizer. It is important to ensure regular watering of these composts. Container compost is usually peat –based with moisture retaining granules and added fertilizer.

Compost and Feeding

Containers require special formulated potting soil that provides fast drainage of water while still holding moisture, air and fertilizer suspended in a clean and lightweight growing medium. Commercial potting mixes are composed of organic materials such as peat, fir bark or composted redwood. Fertilizers, compost, and trace materials are sometimes added as well. One of the particular advantages of container gardening is that different mixes can be brought in for different plants, so that each plant can have the growing environment they thrive in.

Soil mixtures can also be purchased at nurseries and garden centers.

You should also replenish your potting mix, because the potting mix in an enclosed container cannot replenish itself in the same way garden soil does. It is also good practice to re-pot containers at least every two years with fresh potting mix. If you are filling your containers with annuals, use new potting mix each time you change your plants.

Terracotta plants in particular need special preparation. A drainage material must be added to the based – such as polystyrene pieces, broken pieces of pots (crocks) or gravel.

Saucers are available for plastic and clay pots, and act as reservoirs for excess water. Clay feet are also available for terracotta pots – bearing in mind that this will prevent water logging but may result in the container drying out quickly. Therefore, a little extra watering may be beneficial.

How to Pot

Sufficient drainage material (such as crocks, pebbles, gravel etc.) should be placed in the bottom of each container so that water can pass through freely, but not so much as to interfere with the roots. Sphagnum moss can be placed over the drainage material to prevent the soil from clogging the holes. Fill the pot without mixture, leaving a one-inch gap from the rim, to allow watering.

Placing your seed or plantlet in the soil, make sure you push down firmly, so to reduce air pockets. Add a little more soil over the top, this time not pressing down too tightly. This topsoil will need to be penetrated by the root system, and therefore can be more porous and lightly packed.

Water the pot, lightly, and increase the incidences until you can see a little drain from the bottom. If the water drains too quickly, this could indicate too many air pockets in the soil. In the first few weeks it is advisable to place your container out of direct sun, to allow maximum germination.

Seed trays can be used when germinated from seed. Place seeds in compost, pushing down about 1 inch. Press the soil mixture down, covering the top with more mixture lightly compressed. Place a plastic bag over the tray and leave in a warm area until small plantlets appear – usually bearing one or two leaves. These plantlets can then be moved to a larger container.

Re-potting

Repotting in most container plants will need to be done occasionally. You can tell if it is time to repot by looking at the roots. If you can see the roots through the drainage holes, it's a pretty good indication that it's time. What you want to do is begin by selecting a larger pot than the one the plant is currently in.

It is essential to moisture the soil the night before repotting, so that the plant can be removed easily the next day. To remove the plant, tip the container to the side, and tap the rim against a hard object. If the roots are tightly bound and difficult to remove, or the soil has hardened, try running a knife along the insides of the container to loosen it.

Follow the Essential Tips:

- Water the plants before you start
- Clean old pots with soapy water
- Move up one pot size at a time (an increase in 2cm / 1-inch diameter)
- Gently remove the plant from the pot, cut off any damaged roots, look
- For signs of any disease or bugs that may require treatment
- Put a layer of compost in the new pot and tap it sharply to allow it to Settle and remove air bubbles
- Place the pot in the center of the new pot, and pour compost down the Sides, leaving about an inch free from the rim
- Gently compress the compost to remove air bubbles
- Add a light layer of compost, this time not compressing as much
- Water your plant

- Move to a light source, but direct sunlight is not advisable in the first few weeks.

- Watering

Watering is also very critical. You should water frequently. If you only water around the edges, it will not soak in properly.

If you pre-moisten the potting soil before filling the containers to make it damp it will settle air pockets and protect the plants overnight. Fill containers to about one inch below the rim of the pot and press down firmly to settle the air pockets. Place in a well-protected spot overnight before planting.

The amount of water required will vary depending on the size of the plant, the amount of sunlight received, the temperature, the material and size of the container. Quicker drying materials such as clay and unglazed pots dry out very quickly, with wood and metal taking longer. Grouping plants together can slow down water loss, due to less evaporation.

Mulch

Mulch is a protective layer of material over the soil, helping to retain moisture, warmth, suppress weeds, and prevent soil splash on leaves.

- Bark chippings
- Clay granules
- Gravel
- Stones

Mulching can be used on container plants exposed to the elements, perhaps a cold dry wind, or when you may be going away for a while.

Grooming and Pruning

Grooming is also important. You should remove dead flowers and weeds. This keeps the plants looking fresh and full.

When a plant begins to look as if it's past its prime, it's wise to change the plants around. Pull the old plants out and replace them with fresh, new plants. You can keep your container garden current with seasonal themes by growing a sequence of plants, such as bulbs and primroses in the spring, vegetables in the summer, and colorful blooms in autumn.

Two Main Methods to Pruning:

- Pinching Out
- Cutting Back

Pinching Out: This involves cutting out or 'pinching' the growing tip just above the node where leaves join the stem. This reduces the excess growth on a plant, therefore conserving energy for the main areas.

Cutting Back: Cutting off thick woody stems, just above a bud, allows the plant again to use energy in the main growing areas, and makes it look tidy. It is advisable to cut back at the beginning of the growing season to allow dormant buds to benefit from the excess energy. Remember to cut the stems with sharp tools, or the fibers will tear making it more prone to pest and disease invasion.

Deadheading: This applies to cutting off dying flowers and their associated yellow leaves, again making the plant look healthier, and channeling the excess energy into the buds.

Consistency is an important key. A consistent feeding and watering schedule, consistent light, and consistent temperature are very important factors in maintaining a container garden. The more you do to give your plants a stable environment, the better off they will be. Your plants will also flourish with the extra attention. Remove dead leaves and flowers and wipe the dust off the leaves of your plants. This will keep them healthy and keep your indoor garden looking stunning.

Indoor gardening can be the basis of a lifelong affection with plants that never need to leave the city. It can also be very appealing for your interior design efforts. It is enjoyable and adds spice to your surroundings. Be creative with it and enjoy the rewards in return.

Chapter 20
Vertical Gardening Technique

The basic key to gardening is to become able to live a sustainable life. It will also help you out in adding beauty to the walls of your home. If you are looking for the ways by which you can start your working to become more sustainable, you are required to follow some steps which I am going to mention below. These steps will make you able to accurately work upon the vertical gardening activities with much ease.

Appreciate your life. Yes! Appreciating your life is the main rule of making your life sustainable. You are not allowed to listen to anything said by naysayers. Do not bother about any comment on your lifestyle with raised eyebrows and try to find your own strength during tough and difficult situations as well.

Take steps to grow your own food at home. You can grow own vegetables by taking help from the vertical garden. No matter whether you live in city or village, replace the spare space and the vertical garden in your home into a vertical garden or farm, grow vegetables and fruits on your own and make your own fish farm followed by learning the way of hunting the fish.

If your house is having a fireplace, then convert that place into wood and store wood at that place. This wood can be used by you for getting heat during winters and thus you can become able to save extra energy which you were about to use instead of wood.

Stop relying upon the habit of always buying new stuff which you want in your daily routine. You can reuse and recycle various objects and thus can save your cost a lot. You can buy second-hand clothes, furniture, and hand tools and by doing so you can save a huge amount of money which can be used in some other beneficial and productive way for sure. The saved money can also be used for paying off the debt which has burdened you since long or you can better make your own decision that how the saved money can be used in an effective way.

Stop buying most of the paper products which you buy every week in the form of tissues, paper towels and napkins etc. You can save money by replacing these paper items with old cloths or rags which are no more in your use.

Analyzing your current budget is very necessary as it will help you out cutting down the extra costs which are not necessary for you. If you are under a burden of debt then cutting down the costs in your budget will help you out in sorting out the extra cost which you bear. Cut down all the costs which are burdening your budget as well.

In order to get a tremendous quantity of all natural and healthy sweetener for you and your family, you can raise your own honey bees at home and the honey which you will get after pulling the hives twice a year will give you an endless amount of honey which is far more economical than the honey which you get from market.

The flowers which you grow in your vertical garden are then can be used by honeybees to extract juice to make honey.

When you are planning for making a vertical garden in your backyard, you can use the heirloom seeds as they have got the benefit that you are not required to purchase them again and again and you can save these seeds for a longer time by saving the extra costs.

Wherever you live, it is quite easier for you to live a sustainable and self-sufficient life without facing any extra problems. But to be successful in it, you are required to work step by step and do not work on more than one steps at a time. By knowing the basics of vertical gardening, you will most likely to take care of all the needs of not only you but your family as well right from your own backyard farm.

With all these tips, you would become able to get rid of any problem which you may face during the whole process which can be related to anything and any step which you take while working on vertical gardening. Your experience also matters a lot so try to use your experience a well when you are going to comprehend and apply all of these tips, I am just going to tell you. Growing your own vertical garden.

Small layers should be edged

If the garden bed which you are using for vertical gardening is narrow or small, you are in really a great need of containing edges at the place. As the place you choose is flat and there may be a chance that due to rainfall or heavy wind, the garden layer will be blown or taken away so its corners should be edged so that rain would not be able to take the soil of the top most layer away.

If your garden layer is large enough you do not have to edge that because the seeds there have been planted by you at such a faraway distance that will not allow the rain or wind to carry the stuff with it. So, you should be considering this tip while working on the garden that in case your garden is small, you should make edges so that you may not face any problem later on.

Material should be crunched

The organic material which you add to the layer in your vertical garden must be in crunched form. This is because, if for instance you are adding dry leaves of some plants as organic material and you are not adding them in crunched form it is possible that as soon as you water the layer, all the leaves, and organic material just gets washed away from that area and all the nutritional material gets lost. So, you should be taking care of this thing and keep this very useful tip in your mind that whenever you are going to add organic material in the layer, make sure that you are adding it in crunched form.

This will get mixed with the soil already present and helps in making the soiled sponge so intact that it would not get washed away while you sprinkle water over it or due to rainfall.

Organic materials should vary in quantity

When you are preparing the mixture of organic materials of various kinds for making a pile be added up in the organic layer, you add various kinds of materials so that it can help in increasing the effectiveness of the whole material. But the tip is, you should use varying quantity of all the materials you are using together. A varying amount of organic materials helps in retaining the original contents of the soil thus help in making your vertical garden more effective and productive.

Make deeper layers

It has been observed that if the garden layer in which you are making layers for the vertical garden is deep, it will help your plant to get more nutrition from the soil and this tip is specifically for those plants which are having a longer tap root than others. The tip is, you should make the garden layer deep so that the tap root of the plants grows in the vertical direction and will get more and more space to grow. In case the layer is shallow and not so deep, the roots of plants will grow in the horizontal direction and it will not grow as it should, thus leading to the poor growth of plant due to poor nutritional input. So, you should be having a deep garden layer to get the best results out of it.

Chapter 21
Vegetables and Fruits for Vertical Garden

It should be emphasized that small space gardening is not only capable of providing you with bountiful crops of food, but also for the amazing taste that the plants produce. The fact that it looks great is simply a bonus.

In order to produce the best plant crops for healthy eating, it is important that you know not only how to grow your fruits and vegetables, but also specifically which types of each are the most suited for vertical gardening.

With this in mind, we recommend that you read carefully the information on seed packets in order to determine the habitat of any variety that you select. That way, you will know before commencing your preparation and seeding if your plant variety favors climbing, sprawling or a bush environment to grow.

The vegetables and fruits that we have listed for you further below are tremendous selections for vertical gardening.

Typically, these foods include both 'non-climbers' and vertical climbers.

Non-Climbing Plants

These garden selections tend to be small edibles that do not climb their way to dizzying heights in the garden setting. Instead, these vegetable, fruit and herb plants connect to root systems which are shallow, helping to keep them compact and therefore are excellent selections for growing in vertical containers or towers.

These plant varieties obviously do not require any type of 'holding' support in order to grow, and are popular inclusions in any vertical garden. Non-climbing edible plants that receive most attention include the following;

Root vegetables

Radishes are impressive growers when they are small and round because they require little soil for growing in vertical containers. The idea with smaller sized vegetables like radishes and baby turnips is to 'grow them in' continually. They are fast growers, so you should rarely be out of supply.

Leafy Greens

Lettuce and spinach are popular growers because they still perform well when impacted by shade. This means that they can be tucked below larger plants that need greater access to the sun and light.

This is very useful information to know. In a 4 x4 setting, you can expect to be able to grow enough organic food to feed your family of four. When you use plants, which allow you to scale the process based on their requirements for sun and light, feeding a family of eight now becomes much more viable

Strawberries

These are best planted up high and upside down. Ever bearing strawberries are best for growing products in spurts, meaning that you have more regularity of them, and they will provide less weight than when grown all at once. Strawberries grow well in containers and openly along walls due to their shallow root system.

Other

You can incorporate into this group plants that include eggplant, onions, peppers, carrots, beets and cabbages.

Herbs

Low growing and compact herbs are perfect for upside down container gardening and can be easily grown to lush foliage. Of particular interest are thyme, oregano, parsley, basil, mints and onion chives. These herbs in particular have shallow roots, so keeping them to a modest size won't be an issue.

In general, you might want to avoid herbs that grow any larger than several feet in height, such as lemon verbena, fennel and dill – these have the potential to outgrow the space that you allocate to them.

Climbing Plants

Climbing plants are the most noticeable participants in the vertical garden. These are the plants that grow upright with the support of structures, including trellises or other plants.

The best plants for climbing are those that grow on a vine; however, others can have their stems 'trained' simply by tying them with a twist tie, string, or some other means that is strong enough to keep them in place against the pole or trellis.

Vertical climbing can occur in several ways. The most common includes the use of tendrils to grasp the support, as performed by cucumbers, or a twining movement as used by pole beans. In that instance, the plant's main or 'lead' shoot grows upward in a quick twining motion from which it can wrap itself around poles and twist through netting or trellis to gain stabilized support.

It is important that as your knowledge with vertical gardening improves, that you gain a firm understanding of the plant types which are climbers and the way in which they will look for support.

After all, the more that you know, the more you can scale and grow!

As with the non-climbing vertical garden plants, we have provided you below with a list of popular edible and organic sources based on popularity and practicality.

Pole Beans

The amount of soil that this plant occupies is miniscule, making it a perfect addition to any 4 x 4 vertical garden space. In return, it will provide you with more than 6 feet of height with vigorous growth of beans. These plants are extremely popular because of their very high yield.

Peas

You can enjoy garden peas as well as snow peas, neither of which require much of your garden's surface are yet will still reach decent harvesting height. Peas are not big consumers of fertilizer or water, saving you both time and money when you plant them.

Cucurbit

Look for this family in the form of melons, squash, cucumber and zucchini. These plants are popular for their high yield of lightweight produce.

Kiwis

These are a vining (tropical) fruit that are capable of thriving in somewhat varying climates, however they are known for their love of the sun.

Tomatoes

You can look specifically for the 'indeterminate' kind of tomato that has a reputation for excited growth, if you are prepared to control it within your small space, as they can grow up to 20 feet tall. They are easy to cultivate and very hardy.

Alternatively, 'determinate' tomatoes grow only to 4 feet before stopping.

Passion Fruit

This is a popular vine for its ability to flourish and because of its healthy and tasty fruit supply.

Given that we have provided you with an essential depth of information about plant types for growing up, we encourage you now to investigate further the many plant options that are available to you for commencing your vertical garden.

We will, however, give you a word of warning regarding the types of food plants that you select to grow.

Many sources will tell you to only select the indeterminate variety of plants. You need to be aware that indeterminate and vining plants can flourish much more than what may be practicable for your space.

You need to consider how high you want your plants to grow in your 4 x 4 space, and what level of attention you can provide to them.

In contrast, many determinate and bush plant varieties have been bred to predetermined sizes and as such can be much easier to manage in certain small spaces.

If in doubt at the time of purchase, we encourage you to speak with your local nursery or to do your own investigation before you begin planting.

Chapter 22
Indoor Edible

The ability to grow most of our crops in containers provides enough opportunities. In some cases, edibles that don't grow well in the soil can be grown in containers. And you can quickly move frost plants under a cover to protect them from cold. I will be talking about some of the numerous edibles that can be grown in containers.

Tomatoes

Tomatoes can be grown in tubs and pots, thereby giving you easy access to one of the most common edibles in our different home recipes. They usually demand lots of nutrients with consistent watering and sunlight to get them well ripened.

You can grow all the varieties of tomatoes inside containers. Nevertheless, the smaller tumbling and stockier bush varieties will not require pruning as they begin to grow.

You can plant a few marigolds along with tomatoes to add up the color and also to produce a scent that helps deter aphids. Make use of potting mix made up of some loam to help retain moisture for a longer time.

Strawberries

Strawberries are another variety of popular edibles that can be grown in containers. You can also grow them in hanging baskets, guttering, or planters that are designed for growing strawberries. The fruit also needs a lot of nutrients like tomatoes. Plant strawberry with a potting soil that can keep moisture for a longer time so that they can thrive. For the best result, mix some organic fertilizer into your potting soil before planting the fruits.

Strawberries grown with containers are usually saved from most slugs. Though you might still need to protect them from the birds, especially when they are in developing stages, you can use nets to cover and protect them from birds. The use of a mulch of straw or gravel comes handy here to help keep the fruits clean and fresh.

Carrots

The smaller varieties of carrot can be crunched raw as part of a salad recipe or having the light steamed to help preserve their taste. Carrots flourish in tall containers because it protects them against carrot-fly attack. The vegetable can be planted all through the spring and summer by starting the season with a harder variety of it. Get the tiny seeds mixed with sand to help in spacing them out as you sow, though some thinning seedlings might come in very handy. They should be harvested in stages by going for the bigger ones first so that, the smaller ones can continue growing.

Salad leaves

Salad leaves are a fast-growing vegetable, and the process of cultivating them is very straightforward, since they are shallow-rooted, making them perfect in containers. In some cases, you can harvest the whole plant at a time or pick the leave periodically, depending on how much you need.

Swiss chard

Swiss chard is a leafy vegetable with a long harvesting period, which is why it requires a lot of space for growth. It comes in a range of different stem colors that also appears to glow with light. They can be sowed directly inside containers from spring, or you can start them in plug trays as seedlings. Make sure the plants are at least six inches apart. Swiss chard is ready to harvest about three months after sowing them. Make sure they are well fed and watered when the weather is dry.

Caring for your Edible Container

Keep in mind that crops grown in containers do not possess very extensive roots. Therefore, the plants will need to be kept hydrated in dry weather by making sure they are watered at least two times a day during the summer.

During the growing season, ensure getting the plants nourished with the use of liquid fertilizer.

Make use of general-purpose feed such as the liquid seaweed for most potted crops.

For the strawberries and tomatoes, the use of the tomato feed that have a high concentration of potassium will come in handy.

Most of the edibles require direct sunlight, but in the case of the Swiss chard and leafy salads, partial sunlight might be good enough, especially in hot conditions.

Chapter 23
Balcony Gardening

Balcony and vertical gardening are an excellent way to make a great use of the space available to you. Making the most of your balcony allows you to growth plans such as flowers or vegetables in a small amount of space. The best way to make use of this space is to use a method called vertical gardening. When it comes to choosing which plants you can use for vertical gardening there is a huge selection, which plants suitable for your needs?

1. Geraniums

Packing quite a visual punch, geraniums are among some of the most colorful and athletically pleasing flowers available to the vertical gardener. As well as adding color they also add a nice texture and shape to your vertical garden and not easy enough to grow. You can purchase the seeds of the plants themselves from most retailers.

2. Ferns

Ferns are an excellent addition to your vertical garden they offer were trailing clumping version which is helpful is shaded spaces. As one of the oldest forms of plant life they are incredibly robust and can withstand the elements which might be set your balcony. While not lacking a visual punch of geraniums, they nevertheless have their own place in the vertical gardening world.

3. Bromeliads

Coming in many different varieties, these flowers can bring color and texture to a vertical garden. Needing very little soil in which to grow, they are ideal for growing upwards and outwards. With a resilience and a long-lasting quality, they make a fine choice for balconies.

4. Begonia

With both flowers and foliage, begonias bring a great deal to any garden. The flowers will last a particularly long time and the sprawling foliage will make sure that there is more to your garden than simple colors.

5. Hosta

Coming with a range of colorful and lush leaves, Hosta also has a selection of white, summery flowers which add an extra dimension to a vertical garden. Great for inside and out, these make a great choice wherever you want. Suitable for a shaded garden with a cooler climate, the flowers and the plant itself will die down over the winter months.

6. Baby's Tears

A slightly morbid name, but something which can be a delightful addition to your home. Also going under the name of helxine, this is a ground covering plant which has smaller, rounded green leaves which would suit a moist and shady place. While you might have a number of wall growers, balancing it out with some ground cover can be an excellent addition.

7. Hoya

For those who are interested in climbing plants, hoya offers something for both indoors and out. With leaves which might be described as waxy or glossy, this particular species offers up either white or pink flowers which can be useful for those who are thinking about a color palate.

8. Japanese Iris

One of the most distinguishing features of this plant is the green leaves which cascade away from the main body of the stalk. Added to the colorful flowers, this can have a dramatic effect when it comes to choosing flowers which should suit your balcony or the inside of your home.

9. Rock Lilies

As a type of orchid, these flowers are an entirely different color. Offering an autumnal gold and yellow hue, these flowers can be particularly dramatic around the time of blooming. If you have any rocks or tree trucks with bare bark in the vicinity, this cane-like growth can really add something to your home.

10. Vegetables

As well as growing plants to look great on your balcony and in your home, it can also be possible to grow vegetables. Depending on the size of the area which you have available, you can certainly grow something which can be added to your dinner plate. Peas and tomatoes are the obvious contenders for vertical gardening, but others are available.

When it comes to selecting the flower and the plants which you want in your home or on your balcony, there are a number of factors to consider. For beginners, it can be worth selecting those plants which are hardy and tough, but which still present a delightful color in the home.

As well as the options listed above, it can also be worth checking through the seeds and plants available at your local stores. While these might be the easiest and most colorful options, one of the best things about vertical gardening is to make sure that you enjoy yourself and remain flexible. But once you have made your choices, what are the next steps in terms of growing your garden?

Chapter 24
Rooftop Gardening

First of all, you may need to get permission to construct a rooftop garden. If you own the property outright, that should be fine, although there may be local planning regulations that could still affect you. These vary from city to city. In an apartment block thing become more complicated. In a condo, the homeowners' association will need to be convinced of the benefits of a garden. Tell them that gardens help insulate a building, keeping it cooler in summer and warmer in winter. A good rooftop garden can add to the value of a property.

Things get harder if you rent your apartment. Even if most of the tenants are keen to start a roof garden, landlords and management companies may need some convincing.

Once you have permission for a garden, you need to determine whether your roof can stand the weight. Plants, containers, and wet soil can add up to a lot of extra weight, particularly with a layer of snow on top! Consult a qualified structural engineer.

They should be able to tell you whether a rooftop garden is feasible.

They may also be able to advise where on the roof you should put heavier structures, such as rainwater tanks, larger containers, compost bins, etc. Structural modifications to buildings can be very expensive but may be justified in the long term if you have sufficient funds, since they can add to the value of your property.

Once you are sure the roof is strong enough, you need to make the roof safe. You will need to put in strong railings, so that people don't fall. Local building regulations may specify railing design. Don't skimp here. Sooner or later somebody will probably bring an energetic toddler up on the roof, so it needs to be reasonably safe. Even if railings are present, a low wall or fence is a good idea, so that items aren't blown or knocked over the edge. A small pot or garden tool can be a lethal weapon if it falls from a tall building onto somebody below.

Access to the roof may need to be improved. There may be suitable steps already in place. However, if access is only be means of a ladder, consider putting in some steps and railings if possible. Eventually somebody will probably fall from the ladder, so it's worthwhile improving access from the start.

Most flat roofs are waterproofed by means of a roof membrane. Putting soil and containers directly onto the roof risks damaging the membrane and letting water into the building. Roof membranes are normally covered by some sort of warranty, which may not be valid if items are placed on top. If possible, the terms of the warranty with the company that provided it. Generally, protection boards are put down on the roof in order to stop roots penetrating down to the membrane. A number of different commercial systems are available, which typically provide boards with drainage channels underneath. Styrofoam™ roof insulation can be used. Whatever system is chosen, it should give good drainage, so that pools of water don't accumulate. It helps if there is a very slight slope to your roof. Some commercial products are designed for a thin "green roof," made up of low-growing plants such as sedums. They may not be the best for growing vegetables.

Windbreaks are useful, since the wind tends to dry out plants. Don't put in a solid windbreak; these are easily blown over. Instead, use a windbreak that lets some of the wind past. A trellis can work well. Climbers can be grown up the trellis, helping to break the wind. Lightweight bamboo screening can also be used.

Attach any windbreak securely to upright posts, walls, or railings.

Generally, roofs are sunny places, but in some cases, shade is created by nearby buildings. In this case, it's best to grow most edibles in the sunnier parts of the roof, although some will tolerate shade.

A supply of water will be needed, since the combination of sun and wind dries out plants. You don't want to be climbing stairs with cans of water all summer. If there is a higher roof nearby, it may be possible to use it as a source of water for a rainwater tank (calculate the tank's weight when full before putting it in). If necessary, you may need to get a faucet and piping plumbed in, so that mains water can be supplied. Watering may be a problem when you're away from home.

Automatic watering systems are available.

CONCLUSION

Growing fruit and vegetables can be remarkably satisfying, but for those with limited or no outside space, it can also be frustrating. Many people hold the mistaken belief that it is not possible to grow fruit and vegetables in a pot. However, with a little care and planning, it is possible to grow even tropical fruit and vegetable inside your home. You will need to carefully consider the variety of fruit and where necessary, choose a dwarf or miniature variety.

These varieties can still yield a fantastic crop of reasonable size and delicious fruits. You will also need to assess whether your property has sufficient natural sunlight to sustain a fruiting plant. However, many plants require very minimal care and maintenance to produce delicious and organic fruit, which can be enjoyed fresh in your smoothies, desert recipes or breakfast cereals.

Many people would argue that growing fruit in a pot is far more difficult than growing outside. The fact is, while growing fruit and vegetables in a pot does have challenges, it also has a number of advantages, including a controlled environment with minimal risk of pests or infection. This can mean that the yield of your indoor fruit crop is actually more productive than if you were to grow outdoors. Of course, you need to ensure that you have the ideal environment for planting. This could mean the need to purchase additional equipment such as growing lamps.

However, generally, any fruiting plant which can be grown in a pot could be adapted to grow in a pot. Once you have gained your confidence with some of the more basic varieties, why not expand your experience and begin to experiment growing even more challenging indoor varieties of fruits and vegetables. This need not take up a large area in your home and before you know it you could have a productive and delicious fruit garden in the comfort of your own home.

Growing fruit and vegetables in a pot does take a little planning and consideration. However, it is certainly worth taking the time to consider all of the factors which will affect your fruit production. By ensuring that you have created a hospitable environment for your fruiting plants to flourish, you could create a healthy and happy plant, which will produce fruit for many years to come. This small investment in time and energy could allow you and your family to enjoy fresh home-grown fruit throughout the year. The extended growing season resulting from the stable temperatures within your home could allow you to produce a higher yield of fantastic quality fruits the whole family will enjoy.

This will generally be far cheaper than the fruit and vegetables you would find in grocery stores and you will have the pleasure of knowing that the fruit has not been sprayed with harmful chemicals or travelled hundreds of miles to reach the shelves. This means that your fruit and vegetable will not only taste better but you can be reassured that your small efforts of growing it in a pot will also reduce your carbon footprint and the environmental impact of your family and home.

This should help you to feel happier and healthier, knowing that fresh delicious fruit is always on hand for all of your favorite recipes.

THANK YOU FOR READING MY BOOK!
I HOPE IT WAS HELPFUL TO YOU!

www.ingramcontent.com/pod-product-compliance
Lightning Source LLC
Chambersburg PA
CBHW081419080526
44589CB00016B/2598